PRELUDE
TO
TRADE WARS

Recent Titles in
Contributions in Economics and Economic History

Multinational Culture: Social Impacts of a Global Economy
Cheryl R. Lehman and Russell M. Moore, editors

The Age of Giant Corporations: A Microeconomic History of American Business, 1914-1992, A Third Edition
Robert Sobel

International Agriculture Trade and Market Development Policy in the 1990s
John W. Helmuth and Don F. Hadwiger, editors

Comparative Studies of Local Economic Development: Problems in Policy Implementation
Peter B. Meyer, editor

United States–Japan Trade in Telecommunications: Conflict and Compromise
Meheroo Jussawalla, editor

Pacific-Asia and the Future of the World-System
Ravi Arvind Palat, editor

Development versus Stagnation: Technological Continuity and Agricultural Progress in Pre-Modern China
Gang Deng

Commodity Chains and Global Capitalism
Gary Gereffi and Miguel E. Korzeniewcz, editors

Global Telecommunications Policies: The Challenge of Change
Meheroo Jussawalla, editor

The State and Capitalism in Israel
Amir Ben-Porat

The Economy of Iraq: Oil, Wars, Destruction of Development and Prospects, 1950-2010
Abbas Alnasrawi

The Economy in the Reagan Years: The Economic Consequences of the Reagan Administrations
Anthony S. Campagna

PRELUDE TO TRADE WARS

American Tariff Policy, 1890–1922

Edward S. Kaplan
and
Thomas W. Ryley

Contributions in Economics and Economic History, Number 152

GREENWOOD PRESS
Westport, Connecticut • London

Library of Congress Cataloging-in-Publication Data

Kaplan, Edward S.
  Prelude to trade wars : American tariff policy, 1890-1922 / by
Edward S. Kaplan and Thomas W. Ryley.
      p.   cm. — (Contributions in economics and economic history,
ISSN 0084-9235 ; no. 152)
  Includes bibliographical references and index.
  ISBN 0-313-29061-X (alk. paper)
    1. Tariff — United States — History.   I. Ryley, Thomas W. (Thomas
Woodman). II. Title. III. Series.
  HF1756.K37   1994
  382'.7'.0973 — dc20   93-28032

British Library Cataloguing in Publication Data is available.

Library of Congress Catalog Card Number: 93-28032
ISBN: 0-313-29061-X
ISSN: 0084-9235

First published in 1994

Greenwood Press, 88 Post Road West, Westport, CT 06881
An imprint of Greenwood Publishing Group, Inc.

Printed in the United States of America

The paper used in this book complies with the
Permanent Paper Standard issued by the National
Information Standards Organization (Z39.48-1984).

10 9 8 7 6 5 4 3 2 1

To Our Families
Susanne, Heath, and Margo Kaplan
and
Mary, Tom, Chris, and Tim Ryley

Contents

Preface	ix
1. Background to the Fordney-McCumber Tariff	1
2. The Payne-Aldrich Tariff of 1909	39
3. World War I	55
4. The League of Nations	75
5. The Fordney-McCumber Tariff	95
Bibliography	135
Index	141

Preface

Tariffs have played an integral part of American history. They were a major issue between the Federalists and Jeffersonians in the early years of the Republic. The controversy over the "Tariff of Abominations" produced the first significant challenge to national supremacy. The tariff became a major issue in the defense of the southern way of life.

The rise of the United States as an industrial power, has been attributed, in part, to the ability of the Republican leadership to pass laws that raised rates on many manufactured goods. Both the McKinley and the Dingley tariffs represented the efforts of the Republicans, the business oriented party, to restrict foreign competition. The Payne-Aldrich Tariff is cited by historians as the last triumph of the business community before the Progressive Movement reached zenith under Woodrow Wilson. The Underwood-Simmons Tariff, passed during the Wilson administration, reversed many of the rates raised by the Payne-Aldrich Tariff. Both the Fordney-McCumber Tariff in 1922 and the Smoot-Hawley Tariff in 1930, contributed to the Great Depression.

In the 1990s political disputes over trade, once again, dominate American politics. In 1993, the controversy concerns the North American Free Trade Agreement and the general state of United States tariff policy relative to such countries as Japan. In each instance, free trade versus protectionism have once again become major political issues. Should readers encounter this book in the future, they will no doubt be able to relate it to the controversy of their period.

The history of the Fordney-McCumber Tariff, and the tariff laws preceding it, is also the story of Porter J. McCumber's political career. McCumber was a typical politician of the period, a product of the political machine of his state, a loyal adherent of the party, and a public figure sensitive to the specific needs of his constituents. In this case, the price of wheat was the specific need that concerned Porter McCumber throughout his career. In many respects, McCumber, a more urbane and informed figure than many of his contemporaries, had a firm grasp of international politics and economics and understood the impact of a high tariff policy. Yet, like many politicians faced with a similar conflict, he followed the protectionist line for the benefit of his constituents.

Porter McCumber was a symbol of a legislator of this and subsequent periods whose perception of international trade was shaped by the demands of his constituency. In this respect, he was hardly alone. Even Democrats who generally opposed higher tariffs became protectionists when it came to supporting industry in their districts or states. Historians have noted that even during periods of Democratic majorities in the Congress, Louisiana's senators opposed their party's position when it attempted to reduce the tariff on sugar. Today's politicians similarly find that the one area in which party loyalty represents too high a price to pay is that of tariff and trade policy.

It is impossible to include all those who helped us in preparing this work. However, our families are owed a special thanks for both their encouragement and forbearance. We would like to acknowledge the support of our colleagues at New York City Technical College and Molloy College. Finally, we would like to mention our teachers who, by their example, inspired us to follow in their paths.

ESK
TWR

PRELUDE
TO
TRADE WARS

1

Background to the Fordney-McCumber Tariff

THE MCKINLEY TARIFF OF 1890

The tariff history of the United States can be divided into three major periods. From 1789 to 1816 tariffs were imposed primarily for revenue; from 1816 to the Civil War they existed mainly for protection but with moderate rates and after the Civil War duties were highly protective. The McKinley Tariff of 1890 was the first of a number of tariff bills that raised duties to their highest levels in U.S. history.

When William McKinley became a Republican member of the House of Representatives in 1876, the tariff was already a major political issue. Generally the Democratic party favored the tariff solely as an instrument to collect revenue for the Treasury Department, while the Republican party viewed it as a means to protect industry. In 1882, when the Treasury Department had a surplus of $145 million, the Tariff Commission recommended a cut in the existing tariff of about 25 percent. As expected, the Democrats enthusiastically supported the idea. The Republican party also went on record at the time for downward revision in the tariff. The country was weary of the high wartime rates and the Republican administration was embarrassed by the enormous surplus.[1]

In his annual message to Congress in December 1887, Democratic President Grover Cleveland urged a downward revision of tariff rates in general and the removal of all rates on raw materials. Cleveland, an ardent opponent of protectionism, was firm in committing his party to abolishing the high protective tariff that he contended favored special interest groups and thus ran contrary to the best interests of the American people. For the next two years, all attempts by the Democrats in the House failed as the Republican majority in the Senate continued to favor protection.

After the election of 1888, with the Republicans in control of both houses of Congress and the presidency, the tariff once again became a major issue. McKinley, who had been a member of the House Ways and Means Committee since 1880, became its chairman in 1889 and thus had the opportunity to lead the battle for revision. In 1882 McKinley had been one of those Republicans who wanted to reduce the revenue in the Treasury. In 1889 he still favored reducing the Treasury's revenue, but not at the expense of yielding on the principle of protectionism. He opposed the free trade ideas that prevailed in most of academia during the period, asserting in 1888 that "free trade ideas had become a fashion in American colleges and I would rather have my political economy founded upon the every day experience of the puddler or the potter than the learning of the professor."[2] An ardent protectionist, he believed that the United States should live entirely within itself and not be dependent on foreign imports. This form of nationalism was an expression of isolationism, meaning that the United States had to protect its infant industries in order to become a great industrial nation. Therefore, at this time, the protective tariff was focused mainly on Great Britain, which had a policy of free trade, cheap labor, and low-priced commodities which threatened the infant industry of the U.S.[3]

The McKinley Tariff Bill that passed in the House of Representatives in September, 1890 was labeled "an act to reduce the revenue." The wool and woolens schedules were the most controversial part of the measure. Wool was divided into the three categories clothing, combing, and carpet. The duties on the first two were raised slightly from their rates in 1883, with clothing wool going from 10 cents per pound to 11 and combing wool from 10 cents to 12. In the case of the first two categories, there was hardly any change and therefore little argument. In fact, all agreed that both the clothing and combing wool rates had been set too low in the tariff bill of 1883 and that the increase in the 1890 bill was designed simply to remedy that mistake.

The entire controversy of the woolens schedule centered on carpet wools. Carpet wool was a rough low-grade quality grown mainly in countries like India, Russia, and Argentina. It was not produced in the United States because it was considered to be an unprofitable venture. It was in the interest of the United States to concentrate its capital and labor on the production of the more profitable high-grade clothing and combing wool than to waste its resources on carpet wool. Thus, U.S. policymakers were simply obeying the economic law of comparative advantage whereby a country concentrates its production on those items with the lowest opportunity cost.

Under these circumstances, the United States would have no apparent reason to raise the duty on carpet wool since it did not produce it. However, both clothing and combing wool were believed to be coming into the United States disguised as carpet wool in order to escape the higher duties. No doubt there was some truth to this suspicion, but the amount being illegally disguised as carpet wool was so small that it had virtually no effect on the price of domestic wool goods. Nonetheless, the carpet manufacturers in the United States adamantly opposed any attempt to increase the carpet wool duty. After much discussion, a compromise was forged, with the carpet wool duty made ad valorem instead of specific such as were the clothing and combing wool. The purpose was to make the duty adjust itself automatically to the quality and value of the wool. The ad valorem would vary between 32 and 50 percent.[4]

Certain raw materials like raw sugar, molasses, coffee, and tea were placed on the free list for the express purpose of cutting off between $50 and $60 million of the Treasury's annual income, which had proved embarrassing to the government. The national government preferred a balanced budget for appearances' sake only. To aid the American sugar planters who opposed putting raw sugar on the free list, a bounty of between $6 and $7 million in compensation was to be paid out to them annually. The internal revenue tax on tobacco was reduced, and duties were slightly lowered on products that were not of central importance to the protective system. On the whole, however, the McKinley Tariff raised the average level of rates in the year immediately following to 50 percent, with certain articles raised even higher. Tariffs on cotton manufactures increased from 30 to 50 percent, cotton cords from 35 to 60 percent, and linen laces from 30 to 60 percent. Duties were placed on agricultural goods to protect American farmers from foreign competition.[5]

When the McKinley Bill reached the Senate, a reciprocity agreement was attached to it through the efforts of Secretary of State James Blaine. This was the first such agreement ever attached to a tariff bill. Under its terms, the president was empowered to impose retaliatory measures on products of other countries that levied unjust tariffs against the United States. McKinley supported the reciprocity agreement with reservations. In fact, he and his fellow protectionists had forged an arrangement with the silver forces in Congress in 1890 in order to guarantee the passage of this tariff bill. The Republican leadership agreed to support the Sherman Silver Purchase Act, providing for the increased coinage of silver, in return for the silver vote on the tariff. After a conference committee quickly reconciled the differences between the Senate and House versions, the bill was passed by the entire House on September 27, 1890, by a vote of 152 to 81 and the Senate on September 30 by a vote of 33 to 27.[6]

William McKinley was proud of his nickname, "The Great Protector." He wanted not only to protect infant industries in America but also to support tariffs as a means of helping industries conceived but yet unborn. As an example, the tin plate industry of Great Britain faced a high protective tariff, yet there was no such industry in the United States at that time. As early as 1862, during the Civil War, Congress had imposed a duty on Britain's tin plate industry of 25 percent. The announced reason for the tariff at that time was that it would stimulate the growth of such an industry in the United States. It should be noted that American relations with the British government in 1862 were already strained owing to British policy towards the Confederacy.

In 1872 the duty was reduced to 15 percent, and in 1883 it was raised to 30 percent. Finally, in 1890 the duty was raised to 70 percent because it was considerably lower than other tariff duties. However, Congress attached a condition to this duty that would put tin plates on the free list by 1896 if American production of this article did not equal one-third of the importations for any of the years between 1890 and 1896.[7]

The new McKinley Tariff contributed to the rise of both food and clothing prices in 1890. The Democrats, who generally opposed the tariff, blamed the Republicans for the inflation that reduced the real income of many Americans. As a result, the Democrats won a major victory in the House in the November 1890 congressional elections. In the new Congress, the Republicans held only one- fourth of the seats as their opponents outnumbered them three to one. In states such as Massachusetts, Illinois, Ohio, and Michigan where Republicans had held power since the Civil War, Democratic congressional majorities were returned. McKinley, the author of the tariff, was himself a casualty of the Democratic landslide.

In 1892 the tariff issue again dominated the political agenda as the Democratic nominee Grover Cleveland favored lowering the protective tariff while the Republican nominee Benjamin Harrison supported the present law. This election resulted in a sweeping victory for the Democrats who captured both Houses of Congress and the presidency. However, McKinley won the governorship of Ohio, running on a strong protectionist platform, helping his party to a majority in the state legislature. Thus he was positioned for a run for the presidency in 1896, with his loyal mentor Mark Hanna already planning his next political move.[8]

The voting behavior of North Dakota's representative and senators during the 19th century on tariff matters did not reveal any significant departure from what we would assume. The McKinley Tariff passed shortly after they arrived in the capital, with solid support from its Republican delegation--all of them supported the measure.[9]

THE WILSON-GORMAN TARIFF OF 1894

It is difficult and generally inaccurate to state that the Democrats won the election of 1892 only because of the McKinley Tariff. Other issues such as scandals in the civil service and defections to the Populist party also affected the election outcome. However, the tariff became a key issue when the question of monopoly was discussed. In 1892 the working class, labor unions, and others evinced a growing concern about the growth of monopolies and trusts in the United States, and in 1890 the Congress had passed the Sherman Antitrust Act to curb monopoly growth.

The protective tariff became a major issue in the election of 1892 as Democrats claimed that it contributed to monopoly growth. They were successful in persuading the American people that preventing imports from abroad had been a major factor leading to monopoly growth and high domestic prices at home. Thus, when Grover Cleveland assumed the presidency for the second time in 1892, with his party firmly in control of both houses of Congress, it had become an article of faith that the McKinley Tariff had to go.

In his first message to Congress, Cleveland advocated a lower tariff. William L. Wilson of West Virginia, the new chairman of the House Ways and Means Committee, had presaged the president's sentiments when, during the campaign, he criticized the McKinley Tariff's high rates and its reciprocity agreement. According to Wilson, the reciprocity agreement did absolutely nothing to increase American trade.[10]

Wilson guided a tariff bill through the House that lowered the rates of the McKinley Tariff by 50 percent. Thomas Reed, the House Republican leader, opposed the Wilson Bill, warning that it would only aggravate the existing business recession. The recession of 1894 had closed many mills and factories and raised the debt of numerous farmers whose problems were compounded by the severe drought. Notwithstanding Reed's opposition, on February 1, 1894, the Wilson Bill passed the House by a vote of 204 to 140.[11]

The Wilson Tariff, which passed through the House so quickly, was delayed in the Senate by acrimonious debate. Senator Arthur Gorman of Maryland, chairman of the Senate Finance Committee led the fight for tariff reduction. A bill finally cleared the Senate Finance Committee on March 20; however, lobbyists for the Standard Oil Company, the sugar trust, the lead trust, and dozens of other businesses persuaded the Senate to emasculate the Wilson Bill by adding over 600 amendments, all of which raised the rates of the Wilson Bill. House schedules on iron, glass, chemicals, woolens, and cotton goods were revised upward. Farm products, put on the free list in the House version, were now taken off that list.

The Gorman Bill passed the Senate by a vote of 39 to 34 on July 3, and a conference committee was established to reconcile the differences between the House and Senate versions of the measure. Since the Civil War, conference committees had usually compromised on the House and Senate versions of a bill, so the final product would be halfway between both versions. In this case, however, the Democratic senators on the Conference Committee insisted on their version, and as a result the House accepted all the Senate amendments. Cleveland favored the House version of the bill because it was more in line with the Democratic pledge of reducing the tariff. He wrote to Wilson, urging him to resist the Senate amendments. But Wilson and his fellow House Democrats ignored the president and supported the Senate version.[12]

Tariff historian Frank Taussig blames the results on the precarious majority that the Democrats held in the Senate as well as the lack of guidance shown by the Democratic leadership. The lobbyists had taken advantage of these weaknesses to influence upward revisions in the Senate. For example, of the thirty-nine senators who supported the bill, at least three were Populists who owed no loyalty to either the Democratic party or its leadership. Aside from the Populist senators, few Democratic senators wanted to make amendments to the Gorman bill, which had proved distasteful to the mass of the party. Given these circumstances, the lobbyists were able to extract enough concessions in the Senate to revise the Wilson Bill upward. Wilson and his fellow Democrats in the House ultimately voted in favor of the Senate version because it represented their only hope for tariff reform. President Cleveland eventually saw it the same way as he allowed the bill to become law without his signature.[13]

The most controversial provision of the Wilson-Gorman Tariff was the removal of the duty on raw wool. It had been the linchpin of protectionism in the McKinley Tariff, and the farmers from the wool-growing states favored the continued protection of this product. During his first administration in 1887, Cleveland had wanted to place raw wool on the free list. He opposed protecting raw materials in general and wool in particular. It was ludicrous to Cleveland that the United States was the only country to have placed a duty on raw wool. Now with the passage of the Wilson-Gorman Bill in 1894, Cleveland was finally able to place raw wool on the free list.[14]

Unlike raw wool, most woolen goods were still protected. The House version of the bill had reduced these rates from 50 percent in the McKinley Bill to 40 percent, with a 1 percent reduction each year up to five years. In the Senate, however, the McKinley rates were restored on most woolen goods except those on cheaper articles such as flannel and blankets. On these, the rates were reduced to a mere 25 percent. It was significant that the woolen manufacturers, who originally opposed placing wool on the free list, benefited most by that policy. With increased competition from abroad, wool was now cheaper to purchase for their goods that still enjoyed protection. The proponents of free raw wool saw immediate prosperity in the woolens manufacturing industry.[15]

Perhaps the best example of the Democratic party's failure to carry out its pledge of placing raw materials on the free list was the imposition of duties on iron and coal. Both had been placed on the free list in the House version of the bill, but in the Senate they were altered to meet the demands of the protectionists. In the case of coal, many states on the North Atlantic and Pacific coasts, which were far removed from domestic coal manufacturing centers in Kentucky and West Virginia, preferred cheap coal from Canada and opposed any duties on this item. In the Senate a compromise was put forward which reduced the duty on coal in the McKinley Bill from 75 cents per ton to 40 cents per ton. Iron ore suffered the same fate as coal, for its duty was restored in the Senate version but was reduced significantly below the McKinley Bill of 1890.[16]

In the McKinley Tariff the duty on raw sugar had been abolished on the grounds that it imposed a tax burden on consumers. However, four years later, both Democrats and Republicans wanted to restore the duty but for different reasons. The Democrats were concerned about the loss of revenue to the Treasury, and the Republicans were intent on protecting the sugar growers in Louisiana. The duty on raw sugar had been a bonanza for the Treasury Department in the 1880s and had contributed to the surplus. However, between 1890 and 1894 both the duty on raw sugar and the surplus were nonexistent.

Democrats and hard money disciples contended that the Treasury had to have enough gold and silver on hand to back the large amount of paper money in circulation at the time. Therefore, Democrats rationalized the restoration of the duty on raw sugar as sound economic policy. The protectionists, on the other hand, including the two Louisiana senators, whose votes were crucial for the passage of this bill, cared little about the revenue aspect. They argued that a duty on raw sugar was necessary to keep the sugar planters in business. They compared the production of raw wool, which was put on the free list, with sugar and contended that wool did not need the large amount of capital that went into the production of sugar. Therefore, since sugar production was more expensive, it was absolutely necessary to provide that industry with some protection. A duty on raw sugar was imposed at 40 percent ad valorem.[17]

If the raw sugar producers in the United States received protection from the government, the sugar refiners expected no less. In 1890 when raw sugar was admitted free, the duty on refined sugar was one-half a cent per pound. It seemed to them absurd that protection should have been granted to the sugar refining industry in 1890, since the cost of production in the United States was as inexpensive as production abroad. With the tariff protection, the refiners enjoyed enormous profits. Given the circumstances, the sugar refining industry would fight to have its tariff protection continued in 1894.[18]

The House Ways and Means Committee reduced the tariff on refined sugar to one-quarter of a cent per pound, but when the entire House voted on the bill, refined sugar was put on the free list. An investigation held during the course of the session determined that the sugar interests had given certain members of the Senate additional funds for their reelection campaigns. However, when the Wilson Bill was voted on in the Senate, the sugar trust was there to protect its interests. The Senate voted to impose a duty on refined sugar of one-eighth of a cent and an additional duty of one-tenth of a cent on all refined sugar coming in from continental Europe. Of all countries on the continent, Germany posed the greatest threat to the American sugar refining industry since that country subsidized its sugar exports.[19]

In its final form, the Wilson-Gorman Tariff was far from the radical change expected when the Democrats took control of the government in 1892. To tariff reduction advocates, it was a little better than the McKinley Bill, for rates on the whole were reduced only about 10 percent below the 1890 measure. In the McKinley Bill, the tariff rate on chemicals was 31.6 percent while it was only 24.4 percent in the Wilson-Gorman Bill; the rate on glassware was 51.8 percent in the McKinley Bill and only 37.3 percent in the Wilson-Gorman Bill; metals were 58.4 percent in the McKinley Bill and 34.2 percent in the Wilson-Gorman Bill; and wood was 32.6 percent in the McKinley Bill and 22.8 percent in the Wilson-Gorman Bill. From their point of view, the most favorable part of the 1894 bill, had been the placing of raw wool and lumber on the free list. The Democrats had stood their ground against the lobbyists who wanted to impose duties on these raw materials. On the whole, the Wilson-Gorman Bill had been a measure that had promised much but delivered little.

Cancellation of the reciprocity provision in the McKinley Tariff disappointed the farmers of the South and West. Business entrepreneurs resented the income tax, a flat 2 percent on incomes over $4,000, which was eventually declared unconstitutional by the Supreme Court in the case of *Pollock v. Farmers' Loan and Trust Co.* of 1896. Finally, the free traders who had high hopes when Cleveland was elected to the presidency were disappointed. As noted previously, Cleveland, to show his disgust with the bill, allowed it to become law without his signature.[20]

In examining the behavior of the North Dakota delegation on the Wilson-Gorman Bill, it should be noted that Henry Hansbrough, who as a Congressman had voted for the McKinley Tariff, had moved to the Senate and voted against the modest Gorman version of the measure; William Roach, a Democrat, joined with moderate Democrats in voting for it. In the House, Martin Johnson, a Republican, had taken the lone North Dakota seat, and he joined his colleagues in voting against the Wilson version of the bill.[21] They repeated their original votes when the Conference Committee report was returned to the chambers without the changes Cleveland had angrily demanded in his criticism of the Gorman version in the Senate.[22]

THE DINGLEY TARIFF ACT OF 1897

From 1893 through the election of 1896, the money issue, the state of the economy, and the tariff continued to dominate party politics. With the repeal of the Sherman Silver Purchase Act in 1893, the stage was set for the presidential election of 1896. The Democrats had become largely the party of free and unlimited coinage of silver and nominated as their standard-bearer William Jennings Bryan, while most of the Republicans opposed the coinage of silver and supported only gold. Although the election of 1896 centered on the silver question, the recession and the tariff were important secondary issues. During the election, the Republicans linked the recession to the Wilson-Gorman Tariff of 1894, contending that the lowered rates in the 1894 tariff had raised the level of unemployment, reduced the level of income, and caused a recession. Their famous slogan during the election campaign was, "We told you so; let us return to the policy of prosperity."[23]

When William McKinley was elected to the presidency in 1896, his first announced order of business was to deal with the deficit facing the Treasury. In the 1892-1893 fiscal year, the Treasury had run a surplus of $2.3 million. From 1893 through 1896, however, large deficits appeared on the Treasury ledgers. For example, the deficit was $69.8 million in 1894, $42.8 million in 1895, and $25.2 million in 1896. Both McKinley and Nelson Dingley, Jr., soon to become chairman of the House Ways and Means Committee, blamed the huge deficits on the lower rates of the Wilson-Gorman Tariff.

McKinley called an extra session of Congress in 1897 to deal specifically with the deficit and the tariff. The reality of the matter was that McKinley and Dingley, fellow protectionists, were looking for an excuse to revise the tariff and the deficit was as good as any. However, seldom do tariffs cause deficits, and the Treasury's losses from 1893 through 1896 were probably brought about more by a decline in overall industrial production and the ensuing recession.[24]

The Dingley Tariff, calling for the upward revision of rates beyond both the McKinley and Wilson-Gorman bills, was acted on by the House with the utmost speed. On March 18, only three days after the House convened, it passed the House Ways and Means Committee, and less than two weeks later, on March 31, the entire House gave its blessings to the bill. The swiftness of passage was due to the influence of Speaker Thomas Reed, an ardent protectionist, who planned to devote the entire session to the tariff if need be and also to the fact that only a small part of the bill was considered for discussion. Of the 163 pages, no more than 22 were considered. The bill was accepted as a party measure under rigid party rules, and there was little if any debate on its content.[25]

In the Senate, the tariff was taken up by the Senate Finance Committee which reported the bill to the floor on May 18 after adding 872 amendments. In general, the bill in the Senate followed the protective nature of the House version calling for an upward revision of rates. Unlike the House, the Senate spent almost two months going over each item in the bill before passing it on July 7. After a brief stay in the conference committee, the bill was again approved by both houses and signed by President McKinley on July 24.[26]

One of the most significant changes made in the Dingley Tariff of 1897 was the restoration of duties on raw wool. In the Wilson-Gorman Tariff of 1894, raw wool was placed on the free list, and many of the legislators believed that it would stay there. It was argued that from an economic point of view there was absolutely no need to protect it. The manufacturing industry in the United States had enjoyed considerable profit between 1894 and 1897, and the manufacturers were content to leave raw wool on the free list. When the secretary of the Wool-Manufacturers Association testified before the House Ways and Means Committee, he stated the disadvantages of reimposing a duty on raw wool. Simply put, any duty on raw wool would drive both costs and prices up, making the industry less competitive in the marketplace. The protectionists wanted to help the large woolen growers in the thinly settled trans-Missouri region to increase their already excessive profits.[27]

The protective nature of the Dingley Tariff was revealed in the duty imposed on hides and carpet wool. Hides were considered by their very nature to be raw materials and as such had been excluded from duties since 1872. Once again, however, politics played an important part in restoring them to the protective list. The senators from the ranching states demanded protection and were able to dictate the terms, achieving a duty of 15 percent on all animal hides. The duty on carpet wool was raised above its rate in the 1894 bill. These changes were demanded by silver Republicans from the western states such as Idaho and Montana whose support they needed to pass the Gold Standard Act. Those who opposed duties on carpet wool continued to point out, as they did in 1894, that there was no carpet wool industry in the United States to protect.[28]

Unlike many of the textile products mentioned above, few changes were made in the metal schedules from the 1894 rates. The primary reason was that the metal industry, particularly the iron and steel industry, had matured considerably since the Civil War and was now a formidable competitor in the world markets. Among the most important factors in its development was the discovery of large beds of iron ore in Lake Superior, the development of coal deposits in the Midwest, and the reduced cost of transportation by water and rail. In 1890, for the first time in American history, pig iron production in the United States exceeded Great Britain's, bringing a sharp decline in the prices of most iron products. By 1894 most crude forms of iron and steel produced in the United States were below the prices sold for in Europe, making the United States more competitive. This situation enabled the United States to supply its domestic market fully while becoming a major exporter. Under the circumstances, there was no outcry to increase the duties on these goods.

Iron ore remained at 40 cents per ton, pig iron at $4.00 per ton, and steel rails at a modest $7.84 per ton. However, the duty on coal, which was 40 cents per ton in 1894 was now raised to 67 cents per ton. Copper remained on the free list as the copper industry enjoyed unprecedented prosperity in the last decade of the nineteenth century. Silver Republicans worked successfully to increase the duties on lead, lead ore, and silver ore as these goods were imported in large quantities from Mexico.[29]

Discussion of the sugar schedules caused a great deal of interest in 1897. The 1894 act had imposed a duty of 40 percent ad valorem on raw sugar, which had been admitted freely in 1890. The principal argument for this duty was to increase revenues. However, the increase was much smaller than anticipated. From 1895 to 1897, the price of sugar dropped considerably, making the duty of 40 percent ad valorem equivalent to less than 1 cent a pound in 1896. As a result, there was a surplus in the market despite the absence of Cuban sugar following the insurrection that took place on that island. Still, in 1897 the protectionists raised the duty on sugar from about one penny to $1.65 per pound. This was done primarily to protect the sugar beet industry in western states like Utah as the protectionists once again posed as the friend of the sugar farmer at the expense of the consumer.[30]

In conclusion, the Dingley Tariff raised the average duties to 57

percent, a new record. More goods were now taxed by their value than
were admitted free. Even many raw and semifinished goods such as raw
wool, raw sugar, and hides were placed in a protective category. Like
the McKinley Tariff of 1890, the Dingley Tariff had a reciprocity
agreement attached. The president was empowered to enter into limited
agreements with foreign nations for an exchange of tariff concessions.
In addition, for a period of two years, the administration could undertake
the negotiations of formal treaties to the same end. McKinley had not
originally supported the reciprocity agreement in his own bill in 1890.
However, now that he had witnessed how the reciprocity clause of his
own bill had enlarged American markets abroad, the president supported
its reinstitution in the Dingley Tariff, hoping to use it to make
agreements with foreign countries to sell the surplus of farm and
manufacturing goods.[31]

The highly protective McKinley Tariff of 1890 had caused a public
outrage that contributed to the Democratic victories in both the 1890 and
1892 elections. When the Dingley Tariff, a tariff that raised rates above
those of the McKinley Bill, was passed in 1897, no such public reaction
occurred.   The opposition, including those gold Democrats who had
supported McKinley over Bryan in 1896 on the money issue and the
Populist party, condemned the Dingley Tariff, but the public in general
took little notice. Unlike 1890, the country in 1897 was enjoying one of
its most prosperous periods, and many attributed this good fortune to the
Dingley Tariff or at least to the rhetoric of the protectionists.[32]

In following the North Dakota delegation's voting behavior on the
Dingley Tariff, it should be noted that Hansbrough was not recorded as
having voted on the final roll call. However, if we look at his behavior
on previous votes, we can surmise that he would not have deviated from
the party position. Roach voted against the tariff, while Johnson voted
in favor on the roll call in the House.[33]

THE GENTLEMAN FROM NORTH DAKOTA

Before they died, many North Dakota politicians apparently decided
to destroy, or arranged have destroyed, most of their correspondence.
Among these was Asle J. Gronna, perhaps the most famous of the North
Dakota politicians in the first half of the 20th century for his antiwar
stance and his identification with Robert M. LaFollette and George W.
Norris in the progressive movement. Still another was his less famous,
but in many ways more effective, fellow Republican, Porter James
McCumber.

More so than Gronna, McCumber grew up with North Dakota. He was elected to public office shortly after the state entered the union in 1889. By 1899 he was one of the state's representatives to the United States Senate, and he remained in office until he was defeated in the Republican primary of 1922. It was ironic that this very quiet, almost unknown senator was defeated within months of having achieved, after more than twenty years of service, his first noteworthy position and his first significant recognition, the authorship of the Fordney-McCumber Tariff, one of the most important American tariff acts. In the course of piloting this measure through the Senate, a bill that called for a return to the protectionist policies abandoned by the country as a result of the Underwood-Simmons Tariff, he fell victim to new forces in North Dakota which found his politics incompatible with their goals. By the time Fordney-McCumber became part of the American economic system, Porter McCumber was preparing, for the first time since 1899, to return to private life.

The picture that emerges of McCumber as an individual is one of what modern political jargon calls a "Senate type." Although more of an independent than he is sometimes given credit for being, he was loyal to his party, to the Republican leadership on most issues, to his political mentor and close friend Alexander McKenzie, the "boss of North Dakota," and to the interests of his constituents. A slow, plodding, methodical man, McCumber stayed quietly in the background, and once again in the modern political language,"he did his political homework." Perhaps to the public at large he was too much in the background and too much of a Senate insider. When the chairmanship of the Senate Finance Committee fell to him in 1922, he was apparently much an unknown even to the barons of high finance of the East. The leadership of that committee was customarily held by someone who represented an eastern seaboard state. Remarkably none of them had thought to check out the man from North Dakota who had been literally "one heartbeat away" from a position of great importance to them. It became necessary for the Senate Republican leadership to assure the bankers that, while McCumber might not be one of them geographically, he was one of them ideologically.

The portrait of McCumber developed by the *Woman Citizen* in 1922 is both flattering and critical. It uses words such as slow, obstinate, noncosmopolitan, wholesome, stodgy, serious, never flippant, and tenacious. It also describes him as an unoriginal thinker who spoke in a deliberate "drawling" manner and was extremely attentive to detail. They describe his general demeanor as serious.[34] This portrait is further amplified by an anecdote related in his memoirs by Senator Henry Ashurst of Arizona, who also mentions his dogged determination and his seriousness of purpose. One incident he describes seems to sum up his impression of the North Dakotan. While presenting arguments on behalf of the Fordney-McCumber Bill, the senator brought to the Senate floor a number of items to illustrate his point about the need to eliminate foreign competition--razors, crockery, and a cuckoo clock were among them. While he was droning on in his usual manner, Senator John Sharp Williams, the hard-drinking, irascible Mississippian who opposed the bill, snatched the clock and tried to wind it up, to the amusement of his colleagues. He set it behind the speaker, hoping to jar his concentration, but when the device fell down with a loud clatter, it made no impact on the senator. He continued with his speech.[35]

McCumber is generally considered to have been both a political and an economic conservative; and if we compare him to Asle J. Gronna who followed a straight progressive line during the last ten years of his political life, he was. Compared to several other figures in the politics of North Dakota, McCumber certainly classifies as well. Yet, there are a number of contradictions. For example, he fought for the Pure Food and Drug Act, one of the cornerstones of progressive legislation in the first decade of the 20th century, he supported repeal of the Panama Tolls, and he supported the indemnification of Colombia for the Panama incident.

Nonetheless, the depiction of McCumber as a conservative by the standards of the early 20th century is fundamentally accurate. An examination of his votes on domestic issues shows that he was opposed to political reform, the establishment of a federal reserve system, railroad legislation, and most efforts to involve the federal government in American economic life, with the exception of those that might bring aid to the American farmer. Most inconsistencies from a generally conservative voting pattern arise from his concern for his largely agricultural constituency.

McCumber was also a strong adherent to party and to the faction of his party in North Dakota dominated by Alexander McKenzie. While most of his colleagues in North Dakota politics occasionally found it expedient to desert the party in order to preserve their political careers, he remained steadfast. In 1912, he loyally supported William Howard Taft in a state that was among the most progressive in the country that year. His support in 1916 by the Non-Partisan League was due more to the machinations of McKenzie (whose political career will be discussed more fully in another part of this story) than to any political accommodation on his part.

In addition, McCumber was a great believer in the law and in the application of the law to public issues. His addresses on the floor of the Senate may have lacked the fire of that of some of his colleagues who appealed to the emotions, but the senior senator from North Dakota believed in laying out his arguments as though he were presenting a legal brief. The scholars who have analyzed his actions during the course of the debate over the Treaty of Versailles noted this same point. The law was McCumber's passion, and he clearly regarded it as the key to understanding public policy.

McCumber was also an internationalist-not an isolationist as many writers have depicted him. He earned the isolationist label because for several years between 1914 to 1916 he opposed American entry into the First World War, but a close analysis of his arguments as well as other aspects of his career shows that it is incorrect. He believed in internationalism, in international organizations, in arbitration of international disputes, and in the application of the rule of law to international situations. Few senators of his era had his background in international law and his commitment to it.[36]

Finally, McCumber was attentive to North Dakota's needs. As will be noted later in this chapter, McCumber became more of a national than a regional senator as he gained seniority in the Senate, and his defeat can be at least partially attributed to the fact that he had become remote from them. However, a close analysis of his career, even when he was losing his fight for renomination in 1922, suggests that he never lost sight of the needs of his state, although this has become the popular historical view.

Throughout McCumber's political career, wheat was an important consideration. To a large degree, North Dakota's economy depended on the success or failure of the wheat crop and those factors that affected it. Among these factors was, of course, the climate, as well as the railroads and grain elevators necessary to get the product to market. As one historian has pointed out, North Dakota is a small grain region in which wheat is king. Pioneers, the author adds, called the state the land of the type of wheat known as number 1 hard. The climate of the area is ideal for growing wheat, provided that it has sufficient rainfall, for the state lies in the heart of a hard spring wheat territory that spreads from Minnesota west and down into the state of South Dakota. It ranks first in the production of spring wheat and second only to Kansas in the production of winter wheat.[37]

Throughout most of the state's history, spring wheat has been its most important crop, growing on as much land as all other crops combined. One of the most important varieties of wheat grown in the state is durum wheat, a spring wheat used for macaroni and spaghetti. Other crops that are important, though not nearly as crucial to the economy of the state, include rye, flax, oats, and barley. The state has traditionally been one of the leading producers of barley.

As McCumber was beginning his senatorial career, the wheat farmers (and others) in the state were experiencing particularly hard times. There was a greater need for agricultural diversification in the state, for the increased value of the land was exceeding the return the farmer was receiving for his crops. Combined with the problem of obtaining credit and the cost of shipping and storing the product, it made the small farms of North Dakota an endangered species during the first two decades of the 20th century. Promoting the means of helping the farmer had to be of primary concern to the senator, and one tangible way would be to ensure that rival commodities, particularly Canadian wheat, did not further upset the economic balance within the state.[38]

During the course of McCumber's career, the plight of the wheat (and other grain) farmers would be paramount in his thinking. As he grew in influence, particularly on the Senate Finance Committee, he became the principal spokesman for this position, while maintaining a "regular Republican" posture on most other matters. This sort of presumed ambivalence would haunt him later in his career when political enemies would point out that he was a "radical at home" and a conservative in Washington" at a time when a new group of farm statesmen had made such a difference an unsavory characteristic. During some of the most crucial points in the country's history in McCumber's time, he repeatedly tried to focus the national attention on the subject of wheat. His behavior in the Canadian Reciprocity Treaty fight, his actions during the course of the war, and his behavior even while working on the Fordney-McCumber Tariff demonstrate this focus.

McCumber would attack the high freight rates as a problem confronting the farmer and criticize the grain elevator monopoly. Until 1891 the law required the railroads to build the elevators, a statute that only served to hurt the farmers, for they had to sell their goods locally and usually for a lesser price.[39] He also consistently favored the federal inspection and grading of grain, pressing this issue throughout his career.[40] He was successful in putting a grain grading law through the Senate,[41] and later in his career, he defied the leaders of his party by trying to hold up crucial legislation until he got a bill giving the government greater power to inspect agricultural products.[42]

North Dakota is a small state made up essentially of small farmers and small towns. In the early 20th century, over 90 percent of the people lived in rural areas. The largest city, Fargo, had only 20,000 inhabitants, and the capital, Bismarck, only 6,000. Wahpeton, McCumber's home after he moved to the state, had only a few thousand residents. In the first three decades of its statehood, from 1889 to 1920, North Dakota had a very high incidence of foreign born, although most of its statesmen had been born in the United States--albeit outside North Dakota. In 1890, 43 percent of the population had been born abroad.[43] The fierce tribal loyalties of the foreign born became an integral part of North Dakota politics with most of the major political figures drawing heavily on their identification with the various ethnic groups. Porter

McCumber was Scottish, as was his political mentor and sponsor, Alexander McKenzie. John Burke, the popular reform governor, and later an important figure in Wilson's administration, was Irish Catholic. Asle J. Gronna, perhaps the most famous of North Dakota's senators during its first three decades of statehood, was of Norwegian ancestry. While today ethnic politics may be associated more with large multiethnic urban centers, and North Dakota is perceived as a rural and homogeneous state, the fact remains that the success of earlier political figures rested on their ability to master that art. Swedish, and Russian groups, in addition to those cited earlier, had significant identifications within the state.

Like most of the early statesmen of North Dakota, Porter McCumber was not born there. He was born in Crete, Illinois, the son of Orlin McCumber and Anne Fuller McCumber, both of Scottish ancestry, on February 8, 1858. When he was seventeen, the family moved to Rochester, Minnesota, where the family farm was located on the site of what is now the Mayo Clinic. He attended the local schools and taught for a while before entering the law school of the University of Michigan in 1877. One of his classmates was a young man from Omaha, Nebraska, Gilbert Hitchcock, who would serve in the Senate for much of his tenure and who would play an important part in many of the issues that affected him.

McCumber might have gone back to Minnesota and settled there, but in 1882, he got an opportunity to drive a team from his adopted state west into the Dakota Territory. When he arrived, he discovered that this might be the best place to begin a legal career and thus put down his roots in the small town of Wahpeton. Wahpeton is just across the border from Breckenridge, Minnesota, in the southeastern corner of North Dakota and would eventually become the county seat of Richland County and the largest town in the county. It is located about 50 miles south of Fargo, which like one of the other major cities in the state, Grand Forks, lies on the border of the line with Minnesota. In 1889, the year the territory finally entered the union, the young lawyer married Jennie Scharning, a native of Minnesota by whom he had two children, Helen and Donald.

He was the leading partner of the law firm of McCumber and Bogart in Wahpeton, an association he retained until shortly after his selection for the Senate. As will be noted in a later chapter, he did not return to this firm following his defeat in 1922, preferring to practice law in Washington, D.C., until a federal appointment came his way. The picture that emerges of him is that of a steady, sober, responsible but uncharismatic young man who spoke in a very precise manner and always had the advantage (or disadvantage) of appearing younger than his age. His first office was that of justice of the peace for that area of the territory. He was elected to the territorial legislature in 1884 and to the upper house of that body in 1885. In 1889 the Dakota Territory became North and South Dakota, and he was not elected to the new state legislature. He had been interested in contesting for one of the two seats in the United States Senate, but others had a greater claim on these positions.

Instead he settled for becoming state attorney of Richland County, running on a platform that promised strict enforcement on the Prohibition laws. He was an assiduous enforcer of the law, but was not reelected to the post in 1891.[44] Prohibition was one of the few issues on which he differed with his mentor Alexander McKenzie, who always had strong ties to the liquor interests in the state. However, even if he had personally opposed Prohibition, McCumber would have rigidly enforced the law; throughout his political career, he would emphasize adherence to law despite any private misgivings. As it were, he generally supported Prohibition, even going so far as to try to place in the tariff bill of 1922 a provision that would give the government a greater opportunity to halt the illegal importation of liquor into the United States.[45] It should be noted that North Dakota had an extremely strict Prohibition statute.[46]

McCumber was unique in that his rigid efforts to enforce the law would appear to conflict with the general attitude of law enforcement officers throughout the state. Elwyn Robinson reports that, while the governor and the attorney general did try to enforce the state statute, they were in the minority.[47]

McCumber retired from politics after his term as state attorney for Richland County and went back to practice law. However, he was not an unknown figure. He had been an instrumental member of the territorial legislature in drafting the new constitution and in many of the political arrangements made to bring North Dakota into the union. He had attracted the attention of Republican leaders and was considered an emerging figure in the state. In 1892, while in private practice, he negotiated a settlement with the United States and the Turtle Mountain Indian Band which provided that the federal government would pay the Indians in installments over a twenty year period in the form of food, clothing and the like. The Turtle Mountain Band (of the Chippewas) had been forced off their land in the Red River Valley area by the advance of white settlers and by 1884 had been reduced to a few towns. By 1891 resentment had grown so strong that the Indians refused to pay their taxes and held off the government for a while before finally giving up. It was against this background that the young former states attorney for Richland County was called into the dispute to help bring about a resolution.[48]

McCumber's early political identification might well have caused some to think that he would make a permanent alliance with farm groups seeking to challenge the status quo. The agrarian movements of the 1880s did not affect North Dakota as seriously as it did other areas, because Dakota was a territory at this time, not a state.[49] But there was an important movement in the 1880s in North Dakota, the Dakota Farmer's Alliance, and it did have some effect on the politics of the territory. McCumber, while in the legislature, prepared a railroad bill on their behalf; this proposal never became law, because of the railroad interests which dominated the territory. The Alliance programs enjoyed little success, and by the time McCumber reemerged in political life, he had permanently cast his lot with Alexander McKenzie.[50]

Alexander McKenzie is perhaps the most important figure in the early history of North Dakota, despite the fact that he never held or even ran for public office, despite the fact that he was the personification of a political "boss" in a way that few of his peers ever were, and despite the fact that he served a term in federal prison. More than any other person, McKenzie influenced the state's early days and certainly "made" Porter McCumber.   One writer states that McKenzie "directed the political activities of his associate, Porter McCumber." Though unkind, this comment is not entirely inaccurate. It may be pure coincidence, but McCumber's political career came to a halt only a few months after McKenzie, who had been out of power but not out of influence, died. This is not to say that he could have brought the state's senior senator back to Washington for a fifth term, but with McCumber going down to a decisive defeat in the 1922 Republican primaries, speculation that he could is not entirely unwarranted.[51]

McKenzie came to the Dakotas in the early 1870s as a member of a railroad construction gang of the Northern Pacific Railroad. He settled in the Bismarck area in 1873 and in the following year became sheriff. Several years later, the Northern Pacific made him its agent in the area, even though he could scarcely write his own name.   The Northern Pacific had more than minimal interest in the territory; at least initially it wanted to retain that status and so opposed the admission of the entire Dakota area as a state. The issue of statehood could not be determined until a decision was made by Congress to divide the territory into the states of North and South Dakota.[52]

While working for the Northern Pacific, McKenzie also began to build his own political and economic fortunes. He connived with the territorial governor, and purchased land in the Bismarck area so that he would profit when the capital of the territory was moved to that city from the territorial headquarters of Yankton. The Northern Pacific also supported this change because Bismarck and not Yankton, was on its main line. The territorial governor eventually paid for his connivance with his position, but the movement of the capital was made permanent.[53]

It was during the negotiations over the switch of the capital that McCumber first came to the attention of the man who was rapidly becoming the major power in the territory. He defended the capital removal commission, a device created to lend some legitimacy to McKenzie's machinations.[54] During this period and the earlier one when the decisions were being made concerning the state constitution, the future senator was also one of the attorneys for the Northern Pacific.[55]

The North Dakota constitutional convention proved a battle between competing railroad interests. Whereas the Northern Pacific Railroad wanted to locate the capital in Bismarck, the Great Northern preferred Grand Forks. In order to ensure support from other areas, the McKenzie forces divided up the state so that each small area would obtain one important state facility-state university, state reform school, state school for the deaf, and so on.[56]   McCumber was a major player in these negotiations, working with McKenzie and his faction. Yet, at the same time, he managed to hold on to some semblance of neutrality and objectivity, and at this stage, at least was not known exclusively as a McKenzie man.

McKenzie did not gain immediate control of North Dakota after its admission to statehood; not until 1893 did he achieve total domination, which he would hold until 1907. His loss of status as North Dakota's boss could be attributed as much to the election of the first Democratic governor, John Burke, as to insurgency within the Republican party. Even after he ceased to be the dominant power, he remained a force to be reckoned with in North Dakota's political life.

McKenzie's persona was clouded with mystery, despite his great visibility and his role as the driving force in the making of the state.[57] From the earliest days of the state he was the Republican national committeeman, and yet his headquarters was in the Merchant's Hotel in St. Paul, Minnesota. He amassed a private fortune of almost $17 million, much of it after he had spent some time in jail as a result of land speculation in Alaska. He was on a close personal basis with William McKinley and Mark Hanna on the one side and with Theodore Roosevelt on the other. He controlled the *Bismarck Daily Tribune*, the dominant paper in the new state, which faithfully parroted his views and reported how well his lieutenants were manipulating the governor and the legislature. He continued to represent the interests of such groups as the Northern Pacific, Minneapolis grain elevators, and some eastern banking interests.[58]

McKenzie's machine was built largely in the major cities of the state through German and Russian Americans, saloonkeepers, and land speculators and his relationship to the Northern Pacific. When the reform elements surfaced, they would find their greatest strength in the eastern part of the state, among Scandinavian Americans. But McKenzie did not have too much trouble with reformers. He was not a doctrinaire conservative, opposed to any change, and perhaps this would explain some aspects of Porter McCumber's behavior--a man who was fundamentally a conservative but not so conservative as to lose all ties with reform elements.[59]

The opposition to McKenzie was composed, at least initially, of men who had broken with him over some alleged misunderstanding or hurt--not because they were attracted to the growing agrarian insurgency personified by reformers such as Robert LaFollette or William Jennings Bryan. Even Asle J. Gronna, who would become an associate of LaFollette's during the second decade of the 20th century, was a conservative and allied with McKenzie through much of his early political career; he owed his initial office to the "boss."

The Populist movement made some initial impact on North Dakota politics. In 1892, the first presidential election in which North Dakotans voted, the electoral vote went to James Weaver, the candidate of the agrarian protest party. However, internecine warfare destroyed the party in the state by 1893, leaving one less source of opposition to McKenzie. The Democrats were a minimal force during this period, which meant that whoever controlled the Republican party controlled the state.[60] Although McCumber would be advanced as a candidate for the governorship in 1894, the McKenzie dominated convention chose another man for the nomination.[61]

McKenzie's power grew during the latter part of the 1890s, even though he was increasingly becoming the "absentee" landlord. Sometimes he wasn't even in the state for the nominating conventions; he did not have to be, for his loyal lieutenants ran them for him and ensured that his wishes (and those of the railroads) were carried out. As one writer puts it, everyone knew he was a "boss," and yet, he was well liked by most in the state. He was an attractive yet a hated figure, a charming man and a generous one to his friends, but a person who inspired fear at the same time. He was even able to overcome his connections to the eastern moneyed interest and his speculation on Wall Street at a time when "The Street" was an anathema to farmers. He represented the railroads and the Minneapolis grain elevators at a time when they were regarded as the enemies of agrarian interests, as any of the few remaining populist agitators would be happy to remind the farmers of the state.[62]

The first two senators from North Dakota were Gilbert Pierce and Lyman Casey; Casey was selected after a bitter fight that pitted McKenzie against other interests in the state. Neither remained very long, and neither made much of an impact on North Dakota politics. Apart from McKenzie, the most important figures in the early years were Henry Hansbrough and Martin Johnson. Hansbrough was the first person elected to the House of Representatives, moving to the Senate in 1890 and winning reelection for three more terms to that body. He was initially chosen by the legislature in 1891, following the Republican sweep of both houses.[63]

Hansbrough was a McKenzie man but, like McCumber, with a difference. He was born in Randolph City, Illinois, moved to San Jose, California, and learned to be a printer before moving to the Dakota Territory in 1881. He established the *Grand Forks News* and began to dabble in state politics. He was one of the leading choices for a seat in Washington, almost as soon as it became evident that North Dakota was going to achieve statehood.

Hansbrough's departure from office in 1909 was not entirely of his own choosing, and in 1919, he left the state for good. Before leaving, he began to switch over in the direction of the Democratic party, supporting Woodrow Wilson for president and John Burke, the former governor, for senator against McCumber in 1916. Hansbrough supported Al Smith for the presidency in 1928. Like McCumber, he appears to have preferred Washington to North Dakota, leaving instructions that upon his death he was to be cremated and his ashes scattered under his favorite elm tree on the grounds of the capitol.

Hansbrough followed the same tradition of nationalism that McCumber later adopted upon admission to the Senate. He voted for war with Spain,[64] and he followed an imperialistic policy in similar matters as well, supporting the more bellicose position in the Venezuelan Boundary dispute, as well as the acquisition of Cuba under the terms of the treaty ending the Spanish-American War.[65]   On one of the key economic issues, he supported the silver standard, as opposed to McCumber who was a gold supporter much as were most conservatives, but not many representatives of constituencies in the Midwest.[66]

The other senator to serve a full term in the 1890s, William Roach, was a Democrat and the last one from that party to sit in the upper chamber until well into the 20th century. Roach's choice came about in 1893 after fifteen Republicans bolted to reject the choice of McKenzie's machine.[67]   Roach, born in Washington, D.C., in 1840, attended Georgetown and served during the Civil War. He moved to the Dakota Territory in 1874 and served briefly in the territorial legislature. In 1889 and 1891 he was the choice of his party for the governorship, losing decisively both times. Following his rejection for another term in 1899, he moved back to the nation's capital, dying in 1902. His voting record, particularly on farm issues, did not differ greatly from that of his Republican counterpart, Hansbrough.

The choice of Roach could best be termed a political fluke, given the complexion of the state in the years following his selection. McKenzie took total control of the state after this selection had somewhat tarnished his reputation as the unquestioned "boss" of the Dakotas, continuing to run the party from his headquarters in Minnesota, and rarely venturing into the state that he controlled so tightly. His chief agent in the state was one Judson LaMoure, who, as it turned out, had political ambitions of his own--specifically the Roach seat in 1898.[68] The Republicans continued to control the legislature, and so there appeared little chance that the events of six years earlier would be repeated.

Martin Johnson, identified strongly with the anti-McKenzie forces in the state, was the front-runner in 1898. The McKenzie people had acquiesced in his nomination to the House of Representatives, because, as noted earlier, McKenzie was a pragmatist and not unaware of Johnson's standing among Norwegian Americans. However, the Senate seat was another matter, and he determined that C. B. Little would be the choice of the party when the legislature got around to the ritual of selection.[69] McCumber did not show an initial interest in the designation. However, as the convention got under way, his name began to emerge as the most logical compromise candidate. As a conservative, close to McKenzie, and respected around the state, he was offensive to no one. Despite his closeness to McKenzie, he had managed to make a reputation that went beyond the dimension of simply being a McKenzie functionary, and he was still highly regarded for his work as the state's attorney for Richland County.

It is doubtful that any of the anti-McKenzie legislators were unaware of his closeness to the "boss," but in this situation it did not seem to matter. Important to them, as well as to the business and railroad interests in the state, were the prospective senator's views on the important issues. He was sensible on the tariff question, supported the gold standard, and opposed regulation of railroads and other instruments of commerce. Important personally to McKenzie was the consideration that he was the right person to break the logjam that was beginning to develop in the legislature over the selection. He had accepted the fact that his first choice was not acceptable and that it would be best to "get on the bandwagon" before it was too late and there was a repeat of what had happened in 1892 when Roach was chosen. Johnson and the Scandinavian delegation could accept McCumber as a "second choice." The legislature, recognizing that the major power brokers had made their decision, was happy to go along.[70]

The designation of McCumber as the fifth man to represent North Dakota in the United States Senate began an even closer relationship between the lawyer from Wahpeton and the absentee landlord who operated out of the Merchant's Hotel. There were issues on which they disagreed, but they worked closely for a number of years in such a way that their names would appear to be permanently linked in North Dakota politics.

The relationship of a senator such as McCumber to a political leader such as McKenzie is not unusual. He was not the only senator of his era who served in some measure as a spokesman or an agent of a powerful political figure or of an interest group within his state in Washington. If he had simply served as a representative of McKenzie and the railroads, the criticism of him early in his senatorial career would not have been as severe and would not have extended beyond anti-McKenzie people and reformers, most of whom were relatively quiet before the middle of the first decade of the 20th century. But what did cause considerable criticism of McCumber was his effort to get McKenzie released from jail following a conviction for contempt of court in 1900. It must be remembered that McKenzie was more than just a "boss" and an agent for the railroads. He was also a speculator who amassed a large fortune through various economic devices open to men such as himself in the latter part of the 19th century. His relationship with the railroads and the banks and his defense of their policies were just part of his efforts at self-aggrandizement. In the latter part of the 19th century, he began to chase gold in Alaska, and it was this venture that would contribute to his eventual downfall.[71]

McKenzie acquired land in the Alaska Territory and began to work the claim before securing legal title. He persuaded Hansbrough to introduce a resolution supporting his claim--a claim that was in reality fraudulent. He was then able to persuade President McKinley to appoint a friendly judge to adjudicate the matter--one Arthur Noyes, a North Dakota native who owed his initial appointment to McKenzie's patronage.

Eventually, a circuit court located in California reversed the award and issued an injunction. McKenzie, unaccustomed to having a court bind his hands, cavalierly disregarded the court order and continued to work the claim. The court cited him for contempt and ordered him jailed for a year.[72]

McCumber, though scarcely in sympathy with McKenzie's plight, could not disregard the political implications of the court decision and the sentence. In 1904 McCumber would be up for redesignation by the legislature and he needed the help of his patron who would be of little assistance if he spent much time in a federal jail. Thus, ignoring the fact that the law had been violated, he began to agitate for McKenzie's release. The senator seemed indifferent to his patron's apparent tendency to see himself as beyond the law.[73]

McCumber was not alone in his effort to persuade President McKinley to pardon McKenzie. Hansbrough, whose connivance had been even more obvious, criticized the trial and the prejudice of the court that led to the sentence.[74] James J. Hill, the railroad magnate, and Mark Hanna also lobbied the president to let their friend go, which eventually he did, after just a small part of the sentence had been served.[75]

Precisely who should get the credit or blame for what must be regarded as a travesty of justice is not clear. Without doubt, however, the matter damaged McCumber and caused him considerable embarrassment when he came up for redesignation in 1904. However, the reaction to the incident was not as great as it would become, and, as will be noted, he won a second term. It was not until later, when the novelist Rex Beach wrote an expose of the matter in a series of articles about McKenzie and followed it up with a novel, *The Spoilers*, that the full impact hit North Dakotans and the leader's power began to slip. From the standpoint of McCumber, however, the issue places his reputation for probity, high-mindedness, integrity, and regard for the law in some question.[76]

Porter McCumber entered the 50th Congress in 1899, and the major topic in Washington was the recently ratified Treaty of Paris which ended the Spanish-American War and plunged the United States into a policy of imperialism. Although McCumber would later develop as much of a reputation in foreign affairs as he would in domestic matters, there is no evidence that this subject interested him at this time.

William McKinley was in the White House for the last years of his first term. The Senate was dominated by Republicans from the East and Midwest, most of them were staunchly conservative and dedicated to protectionism, the gold standard, support for business, and noninterference with the economy. Among the leaders of the Senate were Nelson Aldrich of Rhode Island, Orville Platt of Connecticut, Henry Cabot Lodge of Massachusetts, Boies Penrose and Matthew Quay of Pennsylvania, Joseph Foraker and Mark Hanna of Ohio, Chauncey Depew of New York, George Perkins of California, and the newly arrived William Beveridge of Indiana. Most of the Democratic senators, such as the colorful but racist Ben Tillman of South Carolina, represented southern states.

McCumber would survive all but three of his colleagues from the Senate. Another, the newly elected Charles Culberson of Texas, would leave with him in 1923. Knute Nelson of Minnesota would die a few weeks after McCumber left the Senate, and Lodge would go a year and a half later. Only the conservative Francis Warren of Montana, one of the first lawmakers from that state and a Medal of Honor winner in the Civil War, would clearly outlast him, remaining in the Senate until his death in 1929. The North Dakota senator would also survive most of those who would join the Senate during the first decade of the 20th century.

McCumber did not chart an independent course in the Senate either at the beginning of his career or at the end. Only when there was a clear divergence between the wishes of the Senate leadership and the needs of North Dakota did he fail to follow the party line. He accepted the leadership of the eastern establishment with apparently very little question. When an insurgent movement developed in the upper chamber, a movement peopled by men who came from North Dakota and other midwestern states, he did not join. He preferred the company and the politics of men such as Lodge of Massachusetts and Aldrich of Rhode Island to those of LaFollette of Wisconsin and Norris of Nebraska Later figures, like Asle Gronna who would come to represent North Dakota in the Senate in 1910, started out like him--as orthodox conservatives and loyal party stalwarts--until events drew them to insurgency. But Porter J. McCumber did not deviate from the principles that governed his political behavior when first elected, remaining a staunch defender of these principles long after such partisanship had ceased to be fashionable in his part of the country.

As previously noted, some writers are inclined to characterize McCumber as conservative on national issues while posing as a progressive at home.[77] The allegation has some truth to it. He objected to government interference in most matters, but he would support government help for business when it came to protectionism. He would vote for the Payne-Aldrich Tariff even when vocal opposition to it was being raised primarily by his fellow midwestern Republicans.[78] Orthodoxy on the tariff question was not the only way he reflected the position of Republican conservatives. He also supported them on railroad matters, following the lead no doubt of McKenzie who continued his association with the railroads even after he began to lose some of his power in the state. Hansbrough, who also owed much to McKenzie, was a "railroad senator" as well.

When he came up for redesignation, McCumber encountered a great deal of criticism from agricultural interests because of his opposition to the Hepburn Act. This measure had been introduced with an eye toward curbing the exorbitant railroad rates that earlier legislation had not been able to resolve. The matter had passed the House with ease but had bogged down in the Senate, where that body watered it down to make it meaningless. Even with this dilution, McCumber could not support it, for he could back few efforts to control free enterprise.[79]

McCumber also lined up with other members of the Republican regular group to oppose legislation restricting work hours for certain railroad employees to sixteen hours and allowing them a ten -hour turnaround before returning to work. He argued that this would amount to a significant cost to the railroads (which would, of course, be passed on to the user) and also raised the traditional argument that it interfered with the right of workingmen to work whenever and as long as they pleased.[80]

His closeness to McKenzie and his support for his leader's release from prison weighed against McCumber in 1905 when the Republican-dominated legislature met to choose a senator.[81] However, the man who ran North Dakota from Minneapolis was still in control of the situation, and McCumber was returned to the Senate, defeating Thomas Marshall, another former regular who had broken with the state's leader.[82] The victory was not without its drawbacks because the manner in which it was achieved further angered many North Dakotans who were becoming tired of McKenzie.

This revolt boiled over in 1906 when, finally, Republicans found the stomach and the ability to overturn McKenzie and end his unchallenged rule of the state. The instigator of this movement was George Winship, editor and owner of the *Grand Forks Herald*, who had once been allied with him but who, like so many others, had fallen away. Also involved were such former McKenzie allies as Burleigh Spalding, a former congressman, who had been angered when McKenzie, along with McCumber, Hansbrough, and others, had chosen Gronna to take his seat in the House--a means of appeasing the now even more significant Scandinavian-American population.[83] Another rebel was Martin Johnson, annoyed at the way McKenzie had put McCumber over in 1899, despite the fact that Johnson had started with the largest number of votes in the legislature.[84]

The revolution against McKenzie and his handpicked governor, Elmore Y. Sarles, needed one final ingredient. This last part of the puzzle was provided when the Democrats nominated John Burke as their gubernatorial candidate. Normally, Roman Catholic Democrats would have stood little or no chance in North Dakota, which still had a significant Republican registration margin, but Burke was a unique candidate and he had the support of a number of progressives as well as prohibitionists, woman suffragettes, and other "good government" groups opposed to McKenzie.

Burke was a progressive in the Bryan tradition.[85] He was appealing to progressive Republicans, many of whom bolted their party to support him. Many were particularly upset at the way McKenzie had forced the unpopular Sarles on the party at the Republican convention. Many of them would demand that one of the first orders of business be the introduction of many of the devices associated with direct democracy, such as a direct primary as well as a corrupt practices law.[86] These and other proposals were opposed by McCumber who had a consistent record of opposing any effort to open up the franchise and give the voters of North Dakota a direct voice in the selection of candidates.[87]

Described as an idealistic, unsophisticated man with Lincolnesque looks, Burke defeated Sarles for the governorship in 1906. Republicans continued to hold the state legislature and this would be the pattern for many years to come--a Democratic governor and a Republican legislature. But the legislature, even though remaining Republican, was reform minded, and some significant pieces of progressive legislation were passed, although the railroads were not affected.[88] Most of the changes were political reforms, including a direct primary law with a senatorial preference provision and other statutes that would give greater teeth to the enforcement of prohibition. Burke would be reelected in 1908 and 1910, and by the time his last term had concluded (he did not run for reelection) North Dakota had, in Robinson's words, moved to the front rank of progressive states by passing items dealing with corrupt practices, lobbying, a presidential primary, juvenile courts, and workmen's compensation.[89]

Burke's most significant contribution was to end McKenzie's rule over the state. This is not to suggest that McKenzie was totally out of power, but with one significant rebuff (the election of 1906) and new devices to give voters a greater say in politics, he was weakened. As noted later in this chapter, Burke pulled the state for Wilson in 1912 and went on to become treasurer of the United States, returning to the state in 1916 for an unsuccessful run for McCumber's seat.

McCumber's generally conservative record on domestic issues was compromised by two very significant exceptions. Perhaps for this reason some critics would argue that he was a conservative in Washington and a reformer at home. These two issues were the Food and Drug Act and the Grain Grading Bill.

The Grain Grading Bill holds greater interest to historians because McCumber, who would rail against government intervention, wanted the government to play a significant role in this matter. From the moment he entered the Senate, he began to agitate for such a measure, and eventually, he succeeded in its passage.[90] Yet, in other areas in which governmental intervention was sought, he maintained that it was simply another form of paternalism. When southerners sought a $500 million provision to loan money to cotton farmers who might lose money because of World War I, he opposed it, even while seeking government aid to underwrite similar losses in grains, oat, and barley.[91] His support of grain grading represents one of the few times in which he supported governmental activism.

The other issue on which McCumber took a position other than in support of the status quo and of business interests is less easily explainable than his support for a federal grain grading law. This was the Pure Food and Drug law, passed by Congress in 1906. For years, manufacturers had been adulterating foods in order to make them appear more palatable, with the result that many of them had become unsafe to eat. Although the House of Representatives had passed a measure to deal with this matter several times, the Senate, influenced by business interests, always turned away. Despite lobbying by Dr. Harvey Wiley and chemists from the Department of Agriculture, the Senate was more interested in listening to the advocacy of business interests. McCumber and William Hepburn introduced the bill in 1906, the same year that Upton Sinclair's *The Jungle* was published and raised serious question about the meat industry (the object of another bill) in particular and all food industries in general. Spurred on by Sinclair's work, as well as the strong push from President Theodore Roosevelt, the bill finally achieved passage. The Meat Inspection Bill also passed. Historians of the progressive era consider these two matters to be among the most important accomplishments of the Roosevelt presidency.[92] McCumber was instrumental in the passage of the Food and Drug Act, making speeches and writing articles on its behalf.

These were two of the few times, however, that McCumber supported legislation associated with the reform movement in America during the first two decades of the 20th century. For the most part, North Dakotans appeared to be generally sympathetic with the major goals of the reformers. After 1906, aided by the introduction of direct democratic procedures, the state elected men associated with reform or at least friendlier to it than was McCumber. It supported progressive presidential candidates throughout most of this period as well. In brief, McCumber was out of step with the voters of the state if their votes on these candidacies can be used to measure their interests and concerns.

McCumber devoted much of his time in Washington that was not related to protecting wheat and other grains, or defending the interests of Alexander McKenzie and the railroads, to pensions. Even after he moved into major roles on the Finance and Foreign Relations Committee, he remained interested in this issue. During the 61st Congress, when he was chairman of the Pensions Committee, some 9,649 bills were called up.[93] He was instrumental in obtaining pensions for a number of Civil War veterans.

McCumber was particularly opposed to efforts to bring about political reform; this not surprising given the effect of its arrival in North Dakota.[94] He was opposed to the actions undertaken in the House of Representatives to strip Joe Cannon, speaker of the House and spokesman for conservative, business-minded forces, of his powers. In this fight Gronna, who would shortly move to the Senate, was a major participant in the coalition that brought about the coup.[95]

The senator opposed the Federal Reserve System Act of 1913. This measure was perhaps the most revolutionary of Woodrow Wilson's New Freedom and gave the government considerable control over the banking industry. Progressives had demanded this move particularly after the revelations of a congressional investigation committee. Initially, McCumber and the Republican leadership supported a plan developed by some rebellious Democrats in the Senate Banking Committee, particularly

Gilbert Hitchcock of Nebraska. When it failed, however, they lined up, with few exceptions, to vote against the Glass-Owen Act, denouncing it as socialistic.[96] He also opposed the Federal Trade Commission Act of 1914, which gave the commission broad investigative powers into the activities of business.[97] He opposed the Adamson Act of 1916, which called for an eight-hour day for railroad workers, and was passed just in time to prevent a strike by railroad unions.[98]

In addition, McCumber voted against the nomination of Louis Brandeis as associate justice of the United States Supreme Court. Gronna was one of the few Republicans who favored the nomination, but he was absent for the vote. It would not be fair to assume that McCumber's vote was affected by the anti-Semitism that accompanied the debate over the nomination. Rather, his opposition reflected his political conservatism and concern over the appointment of a judicial activist to the court.[99]

McCumber would serve most of his 24-year career with just two other senators from North Dakota, Hansbrough and Gronna. Gronna has achieved more fame than either of the other two. Although Gronna was initially tied, albeit somewhat loosely, to the McKenzie machine, he was chosen primarily because of his support from the very considerable Scandinavian-American constituency for the Republican nomination for the House of Representatives in 1904.[100] He was reelected in 1906 and again in 1908 before going on to the Senate in 1910. Not until the latter phases of his House service began was he identified as a reformer; his most noteworthy accomplishment was his role in the revolt against Speaker Cannon.[101] Largely because of this role, he reached the Senate with the reputation of being a progressive.

A big, gruff, plain-spoken man who never lost the manners of a farmer, Gronna appeals to many historians as a colorful figure, although they usually relegate him to a supporting role behind the more charismatic personalities of LaFollette and Norris. Sometimes, both historians and his peers put him down as a willing and compliant "tool" for these two men. It is not the purpose of this study to debate this question or to take a position on it. Rather, it is his relationship to McCumber that is under examination. On the surface, the two men would appear to be direct opposites, yet in many respects, their voting records and their interests were not as far apart as we might imagine. Both men had similar positions on the two tariff matters that arose during their tenure and on the Canadian Reciprocity Treaty as well. Both, as we will see, were strong opponents of intervention in the European war for much of the period up to the last months before American entrance. In summary, although there were differences in style and in emphasis-- and although each regarded the other with something less than warmth and affection--both were genuinely concerned about the farmers of their state.   Each purported to find in his individual political behavior whatever was truly in the best interests of these farmers.

Gronna's Senate opportunity came in 1909, shortly after he had taken his seat for another term in the House of Representatives.   The incumbent senator, Martin Johnson, had died.   Johnson, a longtime figure in North Dakota politics and, as previously noted, a man with good ties to the Scandinavian community, had been a congressman in the last decade of the 19th century.   Like Gronna, he had been acceptable to McKenzie because of the need to placate Scandinavian Americans who did not accept his leadership the way other groups did.   He aspired to the Senate several times, but the imposing figures of Hansbrough and McCumber seemed to block his way.   Then in 1907, Hansbrough proclaimed that he would not seek redesignation.[102]   However, the incumbent changed his mind after the first preferential senatorial primary in the history of the state.[103]   Hansbrough announced then that he was a candidate for the designation by the legislature, even though the choice of the Republican-dominated legislature should have gone to Johnson who had defeated Thomas Marshall for the honor.

Hansbrough claimed that there was a serious question about just how binding the effect of the primary was.   McCumber supported the idea that the legislature was bound to choose the winner of the primary, even though there was some talk at the time that he was part of a ploy to put Hansbrough over.   Gronna also supported this interpretation, alleging that McKenzie and McCumber had concocted a "plot" by which Johnson would agree to be a "regular" and thus give McCumber, who was up for redesignation in 1910, the chance to pose as a reformer and gain some support from the growing reform elements in the state.[104]

On the first ballot, Marshall led the voting in the legislature, with Johnson second and Hansbrough third.   McCumber was the most prominent spokesman for Johnson.   Many Republicans alleged that the question of just whom to pick was open to question because enough Democrats had crossed over so as to raise the question as to whether Johnson was truly the party's choice.

W. W. Phillips, Gronna's biographer, contends that the politics of this particular event in North Dakota history became an extremely powerful consideration in transforming his subject into a reformer.[105] This may have been true, but Gronna had apparently been traveling in this direction for some time and was certainly clear of McKenzie's influence by 1910.   In any event, the North Dakota legislature weighed all the arguments very carefully and then proceeded to select Johnson for the Senate seat, despite Hansbrough's objections.   However, the newly elected senator did not have long to enjoy the attainment of his life's ambition, for he died in October of that year.   Governor Burke would fill his seat with two Democrats, first Fountain Thompson and then William

Purcell, a lawyer who had frequently appeared against McCumber in court cases until 1910.[106]

The year 1910 was an important one in North Dakota politics. McKenzie's influence was waning, although he still retained enough strength that he could not be ignored. McCumber was up for redesignation (his was to be the six-year term, and the other designation by the legislature would be for the unexpired portion of Johnson's term), and he was under fire for having supported Payne-Aldrich, the rule of Speaker Cannon, and other conservative policies as well. The question of the composition of the legislature was in doubt, for Burke was seeking still another term and his popularity was growing. Democrats running for the state legislature could attach themselves to his coattails and win seats that they normally might not expect to win. McCumber could win the preferential primary and still find himself denied another term in the Senate by the legislature.

McCumber's vulnerability in 1910 was considerable, and a more formidable candidate in the primary might have toppled him. Even as he pressed his progressive credentials on such matters as the Pure Food and Drug Act and on grain inspection, he found himself under attack for his views on the tariff and his generally conservative posture on most other matters. It is little wonder that, upon redesignation, he became such a fierce opponent of the Canadian Reciprocity Treaty.

McCumber's opponent in the primary was Thomas Marshall, another former McKenzie man who had broken with his one-time leader and who now identified with the anti-McKenzie (but not necessarily reform) movement.[107] He was the same man whom Johnson had defeated for the nomination in 1908. McCumber won by a narrow margin, 26,441 to 25,208, while Gronna, running for the short term, swamped his opponent. One progressive, Henry Helgesen, and one moderate, Louis Hanna, were elected to the House.[108] John Burke again won the governorship by a significant margin but his coattails did not materialize for other Democrats. Thus, the legislature remained solidly Republican, and McCumber's redesignation was assured.

The year 1910 further marked the decline of McKenzie's influence. He had managed to weather the storm over his Alaskan land dealings and the scandal attached to this matter, but he was finding it extremely difficult to counter the charges of being an absentee boss operating out of a Minneapolis hotel. He was also finding it difficult, in view of the rising insurgency on the North Dakota plains, to counter the effect of being a spokesman for the railroads and other conservative interests.

By January, 1911, even more ominous problems for McKenzie and McCumber were beginning to appear. Theodore Roosevelt had returned and, after having taken stock of his party, which had been decimated by the congressional results of 1910, was beginning to talk about reentering politics. Louis Hanna immediately announced for him, while Gronna indicated that he preferred the earlier progressive in the race, LaFollette.[109]

NOTES

1. Margaret Leech, *In the Days of McKinley* (New York: Harper Brothers, 1959), p. 37.

2. Ibid., p. 24.

3. Ibid., pp. 36-37.

4. F. W. Taussig, *The Tariff History of the United States* (New York: G. P. Putnam's Sons, 1910), pp. 256-259.

5. Ibid., pp. 256-257; Leech, p. 45; Gilbert Fite and Jim Reese, *An Economic History of the United States* (Boston: Houghton, 1973), pp. 329-330.

6. Leech, p. 47; Gary Walton and Ross M. Robertson, *History of the American Economy* (New York: Harcourt Brace Jovanovich, 1983) p. 480; *New York Times,* September 28, 1890, p. 1; *New York Times*, October 1, 1890, p. 1.

7. Taussig, pp. 272-274; Leech, p. 45.

8. Fite and Reese, pp. 329-330; Taussig, pp. 284-285.

9. For the House vote see the *Congressional Record*, 51st Congress, September 27, 1890, and for the Senate vote, September 30, 1890.

10. Allan Nevins, *Grover Cleveland* (New York: Dodd Mead, 1934), p.499.

11. Ibid., pp. 566-567; Leech, pp. 60-61.

12. Taussig, pp. 289-290.

13. Ibid., p. 290.

14. Ibid., pp. 291-292.

15. Ibid., pp. 293-296.

16. Ibid., pp. 298-299.

17. Ibid., pp. 305-309.

18. Ibid., p. 312.

19. Ibid., pp. 312-313.

20. Nevins, pp. 573-587; Taussig, pp. 315-318; James Primm, *The American Experience* (Saint Charles, Missouri: Forum Press, 1975), II, pp. 270-301.

21. For the House vote, see *Congressional Record*, 53rd Congress, February 1, 1894, and for the Senate vote, July 3, 1894.

22. H. S. Merrill, *Bourbon Leader: Grover Cleveland and the Democratic Party* (Boston: Little, Brown, 1957), pp. 187-190.

23. Taussig, p. 323.

24. Ibid., pp. 324-325; Leech, pp. 60-61.

25. Taussig, pp. 326-327.

26. Ibid., pp. 327-328.

27. Ibid., pp. 329-330.

28. Ibid., pp. 331-333.

29. Ibid., pp. 341-346.

30. Ibid., pp.348-349.

31. Primm, II, p. 270.

32. Leech, pp. 60-61 and 142.

33. For the House vote, see the *Congressional Record*, 55th Congress, March 31, 1897 and for the Senate vote, July 7, 1897.

34. *New York Times*, April 16, 1923, VIII, p. 13.

35. Henry Ashurst, *A Many Colored Toga: The Diary of Henry Fountain Ashurst* (Tucson, Arizona: University of Arizona Press, 1962), pp. 171-172.

36. Paul Morrison, "The Position of Senators from North Dakota on Isolation, 1889-1920, " Ph.D. thesis, University of Colorado, 1954, p. 329.

37. Elwyn Robinson, *A History of North Dakota* (Lincoln: University of Nebraska Press, 1966), pp. 10-11.

38. Ibid., pp. 250-251.

39. Charles Glaab, "John Burke and the North Dakota Progressive Movement," M.A., University of North Dakota, 1952, pp. 12-13.

40. W. W. Phillips, "Asle J. Gronna; Self-Made Man of the Plains," Ph.D. thesis, University of Missouri, 1958, p. 192.

41. Robinson, pp. 256 and 257.

42. *New York Times*, May 3, 1919, V, p. 4.

43. Wayne Cole, *Senator Gerald Nye and American Foreign Relations* (Minneapolis: University of Minnesota Press, 1962), pp. 24-25; Glaab, pp. 16-17; Robinson, p. 146.

44. Background material for McCumber and others, most of whom had very brief political careers, can be found in the *Dictionary of American Biography* as well as the biographical directory of members of Congress. For McCumber, in the case of the former citation, the reader is directed to Supplement 1, pp. 525-526. See also Morrison, pp. 80 et seq.

45. *New York Times*, April 10, 1922, p. 1.

46. Lewis Crawford, *History of North Dakota*, vol. I (Chicago: American Historical Society, 1931), p. 370.

47. Robinson, p. 258.

48. Ibid., pp. 147-148.

49. Russell Nye, *Midwestern Progressive Politics* (East Lansing: Michigan State University Press, 1959), p. 288.

50. Robinson, p. 207.

51. Kenneth Carey, "Alexander McKenzie, Boss of North Dakota," M.A., University of North Dakota, 1949, p. 54.

52. Robinson, pp. 198-202.

53. Ibid., p. 200; see also Carey, pp. 4-6 and Morrison, pp. 42 et seq.

54. Phillips, p. 77.

55. David Baglien, "The McKenzie Era: A Political History of North Dakota from 1880-1920," M.A., North Dakota State University, 1955, pp. 50-52.

56. Robinson, pp. 208-212.

57. Carey, pp. 19-23.

58. Phillips, pp. 66-78 and Glaab, p. 45.

59. Robinson, pp. 256-257.

60. Ibid., pp. 222-224.

61. Baglien, p. 71.

62. Charles Glaab, "North Dakota vs. McKenzie," *North Dakota Quarterly* (Fall, 1956): 101-109. See also Carey, pp. 27 et seq. and Robinson, p. 231.

63. Morrison, p. 45 et seq.

64. Ibid., pp. 90 et seq.

65. Ibid.

66. Ibid., p. 82.

67. Ibid., pp. 45 et seq.

68. Carey, pp. 29-31.

69. Morrison, pp. 78-82 and Baglien, pp. 75-80.

70. Morrison, p. 82; Baglien, pp. 75-80; Carey, pp. 29-31.

71. Glaab, "Burke," pp. 52-56.

72. Ibid., 54-56. One of the lawyers who pressed the case for Alaska miners was Key Pittman, later to be one of McCumber's colleagues on the Foreign Relations Bill. See Betty Glad, *Key Pittman: The Tragedy of a Senate Insider* (New York: Columbia University Press, 1986), pp. 19-20.

73. Baglien, pp. 88 et seq.

74. Carey, pp. 32 et seq.

75. Robinson, p. 265.

76. Glaab, "Burke," pp. 52-54.

77. *New York Times*, June 12, 1922, p. 17.

78. For a list of the insurgent Republicans who opposed the bill, see James Holt, *Congressional Insurgents and the Party System* (Cambridge, Massachusetts: Harvard University Press, 1967), p. 30.

79. Glaab, "Burke," p. 5; See also Glaab, "McKenzie," pp. 104-105.

80. David Grayson Phillips, *The Treason of the Senate* (Chicago: Quadrangle Books, 1964), pp. 209-212.

81. Baglien, pp. 118-126.

82. Morrison, p. 154.

83. Charles Glaab, "The Failure of North Dakota Progressivism," *Mid America* (October, 1957): 195-202. See also Glaab, "McKenzie," pp. 103-104.

84. Glaab, "McKenzie," pp. 103-104.

85. Glaab, "Failure of Progressivism," pp. 195-202 and "McKenzie," pp. 106-108.

86. Usher Burdick, *Farmer Political Action in North Dakota* (Baltimore: Wirth Brothers, 1944), pp. 58-64 and Robinson pp. 266-268.

87. Morrison, p. 161.

88. Glaab, "Failure of Progressivism," pp. 195-202 and "Burke," pp. 85 et seq.

89. Robinson, pp. 266-268.

90. Phillips, "Gronna," p. 192. See also Morrison, pp. 212-217.

91. Dewey Grantham, *Hoke Smith and the Politics of the New South* (Baton Rouge: Louisiana State University Press, 1958), p. 280.

92. George Mowry, *The Era of Theodore Roosevelt* (New York: Harper and Brothers, 1958), pp. 207-208.

93. Grantham, pp. 221-225.

94. Morrison, p. 161 and Glaab, "Burke," p. 56.

95. Glaab, "Burke," pp. 142-148.

96. *Congressional Record*, December 19, 1913 (63rd Congress).

97. *Congressional Record*, August 5, 1914 (63rd Congress).

98. *Congressional Record*, September 2, 1916 (64th Congress).

99. Thomas Karfunkel and Thomas Ryley, *The Jewish Seat: Anti-Semitism and the Appointment of Jews to the Supreme Court* (Hicksville, New York: Exposition University Press, 1978), p. 58.

100. Baglien, p. 117.

101. Richard Neuberger and Stephen Kahn, *Integrity: The Life of George W. Norris* (New York: Vanguard Press, 1937), p. 33.

102. Glaab, "McKenzie," pp. 107-110.

103. Crawford, vol. I, p. 401 and Morrison, pp. 150 et seq.

104. Glaab, "Burke," pp. 123-124.

105. Phillips, "Gronna," pp. 262-266.

106. Morrison, pp. 150 et seq.

107. Glaab, "Burke," pp. 139-140.

108. Phillips, "Gronna," pp. 294-299.

109. Richard Norman, "The Election of 1912 and the Progressive Party of North Dakota," M.A. thesis, University of North Dakota, 1950, pp. 28-33 and Robinson, pp. 267-269.

2

The Payne-Aldrich Tariff of 1909

In 1906 when William Howard Taft was secretary of war in the Theodore Roosevelt administration, he delivered a speech in Bath, Maine, calling for the downward revision of the Dingley Tariff--a tariff that had been on the books longer than any other in American history. Unlike many of his fellow conservative Republicans who wanted to leave the Dingley Tariff unchanged, Taft believed that business conditions had changed considerably since 1897 to warrant a downward revision. As a result of mergers and business combinations, the country was now enjoying, a general prosperity that was believed to have been caused by the Dingley Tariff. However, some, including Taft, were concerned about the number of mergers that were taking place and the effects of these combinations on the United States'competitive position. He wanted to slow down the merger movement, and, he saw a lower tariff as the means to his goal. Thanks to his influence at the Republican National Convention in 1908 where he won the nomination, this proposal became part of the platform calling for tariff revision. The preamble of the plank read: "In all protective legislation the true principle of protection is best maintained by the imposition of such duties as will equal the difference between the cost of production at home and abroad, together with a reasonable profit to American industries."[1]

In interpreting the plank, it would at first appear that the Republicans were now opposed to any special favors and protection and wanted only an equalization of conditions. However, this clause was protectionist by its very nature. For instance, a country that was guaranteed both "cost of production" and "reasonable profits" as part of its tariff law was capable of producing any commodity without concern. Good pineapples could be grown in Maine if the duty imposed was sufficient to equal the cost of production between the growers in Maine and those in more favorable climates. Taft and the antiprotectionists were in for a long and hard fight in the coming months on the issue of tariff reduction.[2]

Immediately after Taft's inauguration in March of 1909, he called Congress into special session to consider new tariff legislation. Unfortunately, the new president made a major blunder in not stating unequivocally that he expected the tariff to be revised downward, and in asking only for tariff revision. This disappointed many progressive Republicans who counted on the president as a staunch ally against the protectionists.

Sereno Payne, Republican chairman of the House Ways and Means Committee, had a new tariff bill ready for House consideration within two weeks. It contained important decreases from the Dingley rates, with sharp reduction in the iron and steel schedules. The rate on pig iron was slashed from $4.00 to $2.50 a ton, and at the request of the president, coal, hides, and iron ore were placed on the free list over the objections of House Speaker Joseph Cannon. Cannon, an ardent protectionist and a friend of numerous special interest groups, including the glove and stocking manufacturers, succeeded in keeping high protective rates on glove and stocking schedules. The rates on machine tools, agricultural implements, lumber, print paper, and sugar were reduced considerably from their Dingley levels. About 200 amendments were made in the House version of the tariff bill, and as most of them were downward in direction, they met the approval of both the progressive Republicans and the antiprotectionist Democrats.[3]

The Payne Bill passed the House only because it had the reluctant support of legislators from states that produced raw materials. The forty representatives of these states, outraged that raw materials such as coal, lumber, and hides had been initially placed on the free list, threatened to vote against the measure. Instead, they agreed to vote for it in order to maintain harmony in the House because they were assured "on highest authority" (Senator Henry Cabot Lodge of Massachusetts, a prominent member of the Senate Finance Committee) that these rates would be reversed in the Senate. Therefore, on April 9, 1909, the Payne Bill passed the House by a vote of 217 to 161.[4]

Oscar W. Underwood of Alabama, ranking Democrat on the House Ways and Means Committee, opposed the Payne Bill. An antiprotectionist and tariff-for-revenue supporter, he refused to give his blessing to the Payne Bill because it did not reduce the existing tariff rates sufficiently and it fell short of producing the necessary revenue to cover the estimated government deficit of $150 million. Underwood was committed to free trade and opposed the protectionists' reasoning that high wages in the United States could be maintained only if protection existed against cheap labor from abroad. They had contended that, if American workers wanted high wages, they would have to accept both protection and the higher prices that usually accompanied it. Underwood claimed that higher real wages were an outcome of the increased efficiency of the labor force and had nothing to do with protection. He rejected the argument held by many employers and employees alike that "the tariff stimulated the demand for labor, created a home market, equalized the cost of production, preserved American industries and the American standard of living." Underwood favored competition to keep domestic prices from rising too quickly and saw both the Dingley Tariff and the Payne Bill as legislation to protect the profits of manufacturers and special interest groups.[5]

The Payne bill was thoroughly revised in the Senate after long and bitter debates. The protectionists, led by Aldrich, who chaired the Senate Finance Committee, eagerly awaited the Payne Bill. The Rhode Island senator, a friend and supporter of industry, and a millionaire many times over, was the undisputed leader of the Republican party in the Senate, and many considered him the real boss of the party with more influence in internal party politics than the president. Working with Aldrich on the Senate Finance Committee was Henry Cabot Lodge who was almost his equal in stature and influence, and together they would lead the fight for continued protectionism in the Senate in 1909. Opposing Aldrich in the upcoming tariff confrontation in the Senate was a group of midwestern Republican senators led by La Follette, the recognized leader of the progressive or reform-minded Republicans who opposed protectionism and favored free trade. Other opponents included Jonathan P. Dolliver of Iowa, Joseph Bristow of Kansas, Albert Beveridge of Indiana and Moses Clapp of Minnesota.[6]

Aldrich introduced the Senate bill on April 12, offering 847 amendments to the Payne Bill, the majority of which contained increases in the customs rates. Increases were made on sugar, iron and steel goods, cottons, hosiery, lumber, and lead. It restored the duty on hides, iron, and lumber, increased the rates on cottons and woolens and provided protection for silks, cutlery, sewing machines, machine tools, and typewriters. It was as Lodge had predicted to his friend Theodore Roosevelt in March, 1909; the Senate had no intention of making sweeping changes in the Dingley Tariff to accommodate free traders. In fact, Lodge went further when he declared, "I think that we shall bring out the Dingley bill with some improvements in detail and classification."[7]

Progressive Republicans and Democrats attacked the Aldrich Bill by claiming that it was written by special interest groups. They condemned Aldrich and his protectionist followers as traitors to President Taft and the Republican party who went on record for tariff revision at the 1908 convention. They appeared to have Taft's support for downward revision as well as the support of the midwestern section of the United States. Newspapers from that region urged their elected leaders to fight Aldrich, "the New England tyrant from Rhode Island," and support Taft. Aldrich, taken by surprise by the enormity of the opposition, fought back. He claimed that his bill actually reduced the Dingley rates, a fact that both La Follette and the Bureau of Statistics in the Department of Commerce disputed. The Bureau provided a long statistical table that showed that the Aldrich Bill levied an ad valorem tax of 41.77 percent on incoming goods, while the Dingley Bill was only 40.21 percent.[8]

The progressive senators responded to the Aldrich Bill by dividing it into parts, with each senator taking a part to debate on the Senate floor. Jonathan Dolliver led off the debate with a three-hour speech on May 4 condemning the high wool and cotton schedules. The senator from Iowa did not pull his punches as he aimed his vitriolic attack specifically at Aldrich. Looking directly at the senator from Rhode Island, Dolliver claimed that the cotton and wool schedules were written by the New England cotton and wool manufacturers. During the next week, the progressive onslaught continued as Albert Cummins of Iowa, Beveridge, Bristow, and La Follette made similar speeches against protectionist arguments.[9]

Aldrich, in a counterattack against his progressive Republican opponents, declared that the Republican party was not obligated to revise the tariff downward. President Taft, who worked for downward revision in the House version, was advised by Lodge not to interfere during the Senate debate of the Aldrich Bill. Lodge convinced the president that he would have his chance to influence the final version of the bill when it went to conference committee. Thus, the progressives viewed Taft's silence during the Senate debate as a desertion of their cause for downward revision. It was also one of the major reasons for their refusal to support him when he ran again for the presidency in 1912.[10]

Before the Aldrich Bill was voted on, Senator William Borah, a progressive Republican from Idaho, introduced an income tax bill as a substitute for the inheritance tax that was deleted from the Payne Bill. The Supreme Court had already declared the income tax unconstitutional, and Borah, with the support of Taft, wanted to try again. Aldrich, like many of his fellow millionaires, vehemently opposed any income tax bill. Taft was able to force an accommodation with Aldrich which provoked the ire of many of the progressives. If Aldrich would agree to a tax on corporations and to submit the income tax to the states in a form of an amendment to the Constitution, the president would support the withdrawal of the income tax as part of Aldrich Tariff Bill.[11]

The Aldrich Bill passed the Senate on July 8 without the votes of the progressive Republicans. It was sent to the conference committee which Speaker Cannon and Aldrich had filled with protectionists. Taft did what he could to convince the members of the committee to lower the tariff rates of the Aldrich Bill, but he met with limited success. For example, he succeeded in getting hides placed on the free list and in obtaining reductions on glass, lumber, coal, and iron ore. However, the protectionists were the big winners. The House had acquiesced on 522 of the Senate amendments to the original Payne Bill, while the Senate had yielded on only 124. The remaining 201 amendments had been compromised, including the one on sugar. Raw sugar remained the same as it was in the Dingley Bill, but the duty on refined sugar was reduced from 12.5 cents per hundred pounds to 7.5 cents. The reason for this reduction was largely due to the public outcry against the sugar trust, which was viewed as the leading monopoly of the period. However, it made no difference in the price of sugar that consumers had to pay because competition between raw and refined sugar had reduced the margin between the price of both in the market-place.[12]

Though the final Payne-Aldrich Bill remained a disappointment to those who wanted a downward revision of the tariff, one section of the bill did please them. This provision called for the creation of a tariff board to recommend "scientific" schedules, the corporation tax, and the European principle of maximum and minimum rates. This last part on maximum and minimum rates would give the president certain discretionary powers. It stated that the Payne-Aldrich Tariff rates were declared to constitute the minimum tariff of the United States. To these rates, 25 percent was to be added to the value of articles imported on goods coming from countries that discriminated against the United States. Discrimination could take the form of higher tariff rates against the United States or foreign subsidized imports. In any event, after March 31, 1910, the maximum tariff was to be applied unless the president was satisfied there was no undue discrimination. Taft never allowed the maximum rates to take effect.[13]

The progressive Republicans blamed Taft for deserting their cause on the tariff issue. He could have taken a firm stand and vetoed the bill. There was no doubt that the president supported lower tariffs and had done what he could to influence members of the conference committee, as mentioned above. However, the president firmly believed that the bill that emerged from the conference committee was the best he could get, and under no circumstances did he consider breaking with the conservatives on this issue. It must be remembered that he saw a lower tariff as a means of slowing the merger movement, believing that the tariff and trust busting were related issues. This president was able to break up more trusts than any of his predecessors.

The Democrats made the Payne-Aldrich Tariff a political issue in the congressional elections of 1910 and in the presidential election in

1912. Underwood led the attack, claiming that the Payne-Aldrich Bill represented an increase in the tariff level of at least 2 percent, while 80 percent of its rates were the same as those of the Dingley Tariff. In 1910 the Democrats, for the first time in sixteen years, gained control of the House.[14]

McCumber and Johnson were the two Republican senators representing North Dakota at the time of the passage of the Payne-Aldrich Tariff. The study by W. W. Phillips reveals that McCumber voted against the Republican leadership on the Payne-Aldrich Tariff eleven times and voted with it on seventy eight occasions. His vote was not recorded on some other issues.[15]   Part of his behavior can be explained by his closeness to McKenzie and other significant interests in the state, and some by the fact that he was becoming an integral part of the conservative party leadership in Washington. With Taft, he believed that this was one of the best tariffs that had ever been devised. He joined with the president and other pro Payne-Aldrich legislators in celebrating its passage. Martin Johnson also voted in favor of the Payne-Aldrich Tariff.[16]

Because the elections of 1910 had produced a Democratic majority in the House of Representatives, insurgents and Democrats held the balance of power. It was against this backdrop that President Taft attempted to deal with the issue of trade reciprocity with Canada in the short session of Congress in the spring of 1911 after having negotiated an agreement with the Canadian prime minister, Sir Wilfred Laurier. When we consider that Taft's problems within his party came largely from the Middle-west, a move such as this only served to exacerbate the difference between the two wings of the party, which now were clearly identified on geographical terms.[17] It had a similar effect on Canada, for Laurier, in order to meet the farmer's growing demands in the western part of his country, would alienate elements in the East.[18]

To the Liberal party of Canada, the Reciprocity Treaty was an opportunity to bolster their sagging political situation. The Laurier government faced the prospect of dissolution and no popular issue on which to fight for a new term. Since 1866, Canadians had hoped for reciprocity with the United States, and now they were presented with what they regarded as a golden opportunity.[19]   Furthermore, western Canada (usually defined as the area between Ontario and British Columbia), and including the provinces that bordered North Dakota, had been experiencing a significant period of growth for many years prior to 1911, and the Liberals believed they would support the measure with enthusiasm.

Canadian tariff policy had been based on a "two-tier" system with a general tariff and a British preference tariff that allowed a lower rate of duties. In 1907 reciprocity arrangements with other countries caused a lowering of duties with those nations as well. The Payne-Aldrich Tariff took this into account when they imposed a 25 percent surcharge on goods from countries that discriminated against the United States including Canada. This precipitated discussions between the United States and their northern neighbors, initiated by the United States, which culminated in 1911 with the announcement that they had achieved a reciprocal arrangement. Included in this arrangement was an elimination on duties for agricultural products and a lowering of them on farm implements and other classes of manufactured items.

It caused an initial favorable reaction in Canada; however, opposition began to develop, which would completely upset Laurier's hopes from a variety of sources. In particular, opposition arose from those who believed that the arrangement would weaken ties with Great Britain as well as from dissident groups within Quebec. The opposition was strengthened by the widely advertised remark by House Speaker Champ Clark who openly called for the annexation of Canada by the United States, as well as by pro-annexation editorials in U.S. papers, including those of the Hearst Press. What Laurier had hoped would be a winning issue soon turned into a major problem for him.[20]

South of the border events proved that the president had greater support in the opposition party than in his own. The proposal required a vote by both houses of Congress rather than the two-thirds vote of the Senate needed for a treaty. It quickly passed the House of Representatives, but in the Senate it met a different fate. Aldrich was ill, and the leadership fell to Senator Eugene Hale of Maine who opposed the agreement. Noting the hostility in the Senate Finance Committee, the president had to turn to the Democratic senator William Joel Stone of Missouri for leadership. Stone was forced into the position by an almost complete abdication of responsibility by the Republican leadership at this time--a body somewhat absorbed with the fight over the expulsion of one of their members.[21]

Inside the Finance Committee, McCumber took immediate exception to the agreement. He opposed all aspects of the matter. He had the support of the newspapers in North Dakota, for most of them opposed the measure in the strongest possible terms. *The Fargo Forum*, and *The Grand Forks Evening Times* insisted that the farmer would be the chief victim of the legislation.[22] Within the Finance Committee, McCumber took up the task of heckling pro-treaty witnesses, while carefully guiding anti-treaty witnesses through their testimony. Such groups as the Grangers argued that the farmer faced a catastrophe if the Canadian Reciprocity Treaty became law.[23]

The arguments that these groups made mirrored McCumber's concern about the measure. American lands were less fertile than before and needed the advantage that would be destroyed if the tariff barrier erected against Canadian goods was torn down. The East would profit from the measure because their manufactured goods still enjoyed some protection, whereas the production costs in the Mid-west were placing the farmer in greater jeopardy.[24] The bill was reported to the Senate on February 24, 1911, without the endorsement of the committee and after three days of futile debate the issue was shelved, with a call for a special session to be convened in April.[25] Taft had to be dissuaded from forcing a vote during this period, for fear that there might be a negative result.[26]

McCumber made one of the strongest speeches on the floor during the debate, although it was not one of his best. He emphasized that farmers needed the protection that they were currently afforded by U.S. tariff law and that this change would cause serious damage. The grain growers of the Mid-west would be the chief victims of this change. Other speeches were delivered by other leaders of the progressive midwestern group in the Congress, including LaFollette, along with other more conservative midwestern legislators. The North Dakota delegation was solidly in the anti-reciprocity camp.[27] To them, it was as North Dakota Congressman Henry Helgesen would state later during debate on the bill in June, a case of the "farmers against the cities." Congressman Charles Lindbergh of Minnesota said that it amounted to favoring a privileged few while taxing everyone else.[28]

Working closely with Democratic leaders in the House, such as the new speaker, Champ Clark of Missouri, and the new Ways and Means chairman, Underwood, Taft tried again in the special session of Congress that began on April 4.[29] On April 21, the measure passed the House by 268 to 89, with most of the negative votes coming from the members of the president's own party.[30] It took longer to get through the Senate. Early in May, hearings opened before the Senate Finance Committee, and once again, McCumber was among the leading critics of the measure. Dozens of representatives of farm interests came before the panel to express their opposition. In addition to the farmers, lumber interests appeared before the committee, although the users of paper, including some newspapers, applauded the proposal.

The measure was reported out of committee on June 13, once again without recommendation. Democratic leaders such as Stone and Williams, were favorable to the principle of reciprocity; McCumber and LaFollette voiced two angry dissents. LaFollette indicated that he did not oppose the principle of reciprocity, but he believed that this measure did not represent real reciprocity.[31] McCumber's report completely dismissed both the principle and the specifics.

McCumber began the debate on June 14 with a savage attack on the measure. He admitted that the measure would pass, stressing the points he had argued in his written statement. He raised the issue of Canadian hard wheat as a factor that would lower the price of grain produced in the United States and the unfavorable conditions that would result if the bill passed.[32] However, the tactics that put this bill in jeopardy were not contained in arguments such as his but in efforts to sidetrack the measure with a series of amendments that in effect opened up the whole question of tariff reform. The Senate finally brought the matter to a vote on July 22, and the Canadian Reciprocity Treaty received the approval of the upper chamber by a 53 to 27 vote, with McCumber and most midwestern Republicans, progressive and conservative, voting in the minority.[33]

The Canadian Reciprocity Treaty never became law because of events on the other side of the border. Taft had been badly damaged by events leading up to the bill's passage. His was a pyrrhic victory, but Canadian Prime Minister Laurier suffered even greater harm. Challenged in an election on the issue by the Conservative party of Sir Robert Borden, Laurier was unable to defend his position sufficiently to prevent a sweep by the opposition in the populous provinces of Ontario and Quebec. With this defeat, reciprocity died.[34]

Taft had to wait a little longer for his political punishment at the hands of the midwesterners, particularly in the state of North Dakota. In the 1912 primary, they voted for Robert LaFollette over the president, thus giving the Wisconsin insurgent one of his few primary victories before he was forced to withdraw and Theodore Roosevelt stepped in to pick up the progressive banner. Taft garnered only 1,800 votes, compared with over almost 34,000 for the LaFollette candidacy and 24,000 for the hastily arranged campaign for the former president.[35] When Taft won the convention and Roosevelt bolted in the party, most Midwest progressives followed to support the third-party candidacy.

The Canadian Reciprocity Treaty was a major issue in the primary. Conservative Republicans, faced with the problem of loyalty to the president, found themselves at a disadvantage in their position in supporting a president who had proposed such an agreement, even though the proposal had been scuttled by a decision made in Canada. Democrats faced an even more difficult problem, given their support of the president, even though their crisis would not come until the general election in November.[36]

One of those who won was Louis Hanna, who had voted as a congressman against the Reciprocity Treaty. He defeated a conservative for the Republican nomination for the governorship. Three Republican progressives were chosen for the House seats, including George Young, Patrick Norton and Henry Helgesen. Helgesen had been one of the most vocal congressmen against the treaty. A native of Iowa who had moved to North Dakota shortly before statehood, Helgesen was a businessman who had been elected to Congress in 1910 and was aligned on most issues with Gronna and LaFollette. The Democratic gubernatorial nomination went to one Frank Hellstrom since Burke did not seek reelection.

In the general election, both McCumber and Gronna supported Taft.

For McCumber, the choice was not too difficult, for the Canadian Reciprocity Treaty had been one of the few issues on which he broke with the president. For Gronna, the decision was a bit more difficult, because his sympathies would have been with an insurgent in that year. Wilson won the state, but by a small margin, and his victory was due largely to the efforts of Burke, who managed to maintain much of his popularity even though the Democratic party was closely identified with support for the treaty.   Otherwise, the party of the newly elected president suffered greatly at the polls. Wilson's margin was only 4,000 votes over Roosevelt, while Taft garnered nearly 6,000.[37] Had the two Republican candidates' votes been combined, Wilson would probably have lost the state. Hanna defeated Hellstrom for the governorship, thus returning the statehouse to the Republicans for the first time in six years, while Helgesen, Young, and Norton took the three House seats.[38]

For the first time in his career, McCumber was obliged to work with a Democratic president as well as a Finance Committee dominated by the Democratic party.   One of the first orders of business, as promised in the campaign by the president, was to revise the Payne-Aldrich Tariff.

THE UNDERWOOD-SIMMONS TARIFF ACT OF 1913

The election of 1912 gave the Democrats control of the presidency and both houses of congress. When Woodrow Wilson took the oath of office in March, 1913, a major test of his leadership in the Democratic party was tariff reform.   The Democrats, being the minority party during those ten years, had argued unsuccessfully that the protective tariff constituted special interests legislation benefiting the few. In fact, the opponents of protectionism blamed the high tariff for the 25 percent increase in the cost of living that occurred between 1897 and 1907. On the other hand, the Republican leadership had been more successful in linking the high Dingley and Payne tariffs to the prosperity of the first decade of the twentieth century. Now with the Democrats in control of the political apparatus in Washington, the first major downward revision in the tariff since 1846 was a distinct possibility.[39]

In the battle for tariff reform, Wilson had the support of various groups. The progressive Republicans in the midwest opposed the Payne-Aldrich Bill and criticized President Taft for supporting it. In the congressional elections of 1910, the American people elected Democratic governors in normally Republican states and gave the Democrats control of the House of Representatives for the first time since 1892. To prove the Democratic commitment to reform, the Democratic majority in the House of Representatives approved three measures calling for tariff reduction in 1911 and 1912.   At the Democratic Convention in 1912 where Wilson was eventually nominated, tariff reduction became a major issue, second only to regulation of big business.[40]

It did not take Wilson very long to move on tariff reform.   Even before taking the oath of office in March, he met with Underwood, who would become chairman of the House Ways and Means Committee.   He urged Underwood to begin tariff reform immediately, and the Alabamian promised the president-elect a bill by March, 1913.   By February 19 Underwood and his fellow Democrats completed their hearings and a tentative draft of a new tariff bill.   Wilson received a copy of it on March 17.[41]

On April 1, less than a month after taking the oath of office, Wilson met with Underwood in the White House concerning the draft of the new tariff bill. The president criticized Underwood for surrendering to the lobbyists, who wanted to reimpose duties on farm products, sugar, leather boots, shoes, and raw wool. He ordered the committee's bill rewritten to provide for free food, sugar, leather, and wool, and he threatened to veto the measure. Underwood, in his own defense, warned the president that the special interest groups would attempt to block wholesale revision.   Wilson was aware of this and similarly aware that these groups had influence on both sides of the aisle.   For example, many Democratic congressmen from Massachusetts wanted to continue the protection of the shoe industry: Senator Furnifold Simmons of North Carolina, the new chairman of the Senate Finance Committee, favored the protection of cotton textiles, and even Underwood had insisted on continuing the moderate protection for sugar and wool which was provided for in the Payne-Aldrich Bill.[42]

Underwood accepted Wilson's leadership and guided a new tariff bill through the House.   He contended that the Democratic party stood for tariffs for revenue purposes only while attacking the Republican position that the tariff should be equal to the difference between production costs at home and abroad, with an allowance for a reasonable profit.

The Democratic party stands for a tariff for revenue only. We do not propose to tax one man for the benefit of another, except for the necessary revenue that we must raise to administer this Government economically.   Then how do we arrive at a basis in writing a revenue tariff bill? We adopt the competitive theory.   We say that no revenue can be produced at the customhouse unless there is some competition between the products of foreign countries and domestic products...and that if you want to raise revenue at the customhouse you must admit some importations.[43]

On May 8, 1913, the House of Representatives voted 281 to 139 to approve the revised Underwood Bill. Only five Democrats, four of them from Louisiana, a sugar state, voted against the measure; their defection was more than offset by the two Republicans, four Progressives, and one independent who voted with the majority. It was a spectacular victory for Wilson.[44]

The Democratic majority of six in the Senate did not guarantee the success of the bill in that chamber. The Senate had proved to be the wrecking ground for the supporters of low tariffs and free trade in the past. It was here that the Payne Bill had been altered beyond recognition only four years before. Simmons was a presidential loyalist, but only four years before he had supported some of the Aldrich amendments to the Payne Bill in return for increased protection for North Carolina lumber and textiles. He warned the president that the whole tariff bill was in danger unless the wool and sugar schedules were separated from it. Democratic senators Thomas Walsh of Montana, and Ashurst were opposed to placing wool and sugar on the free list, an integral part of the Underwood Bill that Wilson supported.[45]

Wilson met with hostile senators using both pressure and praise to convince them to honor the Democratic pledge of a lower tariff. However, it was the hordes of lobbyists that Wilson had to defeat. He told reporters that Washington was so filled with lobbyists that "a brick couldn't be thrown without hitting one of them." He threatened to reveal both their existence and influence to the public, hoping to embarrass both the lobbyists and those senators who yielded to them. He said:

I think that the public ought to know the extraordinary exertions being made by the lobby in Washington to gain recognition for certain alterations in the tariff bill.... It is of serious interest to the country that the people at large should have no lobby and be voiceless in these matters, while great bodies of astute men seek to create an artificial opinion and to overcome the interests of the public for their private profit.[46]

This tactic proved successful as Cummins introduced a resolution, on May 27, to provide for a select committee of five senators to investigate the alleged lobby. Cummins's move was more to embarrass the Democrats by forcing them to block the investigation or to allow it to proceed and prove that Wilson's charges were groundless. Wilson supported the resolution, and Democratic Senator James Reed of Missouri amended it by suggesting that all senators disclose their property holdings or financial interests that might be affected by the new tariff legislation. A subcommittee of the Judiciary Committee initiated the investigation that began on June 2, 1913. One by one, senators came before the subcommittee to reveal their wealth, financial interests, and relationship to the lobbyists. When this part of the investigation was completed on June 9, it was the lobbyists' turn to testify. During that part of the hearings, it was discovered that the beet sugar manufacturers had spent $5 million during the preceding twenty years to enlist politicians, businessmen, and bankers in the fight against free sugar.[47]

The passage of this resolution and subsequent hearings not only assured the success of the Underwood Bill in the Senate but also unmasked the workings of the lobby in the Congress. LaFollette, who had previously criticized Wilson for making the Underwood Bill a partisan measure, now praised him for his fight against the lobby. LaFollette wrote that "the country is indebted to President Wilson for exploding the bomb that blew the lid off the congressional lobby."[48]

The Underwood-Simmons Bill was voted on in the Senate on September 9, 1913 where it passed by a vote of 44 to 37. While it is incidental to the study of tariff reform, it should be noted that many historians attribute virtual united Republican opposition to the Underwood-Simmons Tariff to Wilson's "dictatorial" tactics in making support for this measure a key test of loyalty for Democrats. This was hardly a factor in Porter McCumber's thinking, but it might well have been for some progressive Republicans. Still, McCumber lost no opportunity during the debates to score the opposition party for lining up at the president's behest.

The bill that Wilson signed on October 3 called for an average tariff rate of 27 percent or 10 percent lower than the Payne-Aldrich Tariff. The expanded free list included wool, meats, lumber, foodstuffs, farm produce, and various types of farm and office machinery. Sugar, however, was compromised. It was reduced from 1.9 cents to 1 cent a pound for three years, after which it was put on the free list.[49]

The announced objective of the Underwood Bill was not free trade but rather the destruction of the special privileges and the undue advantage that Democrats contended Republican protectionist policy had conferred on American producers. The average ad valorem rate of the Payne-Aldrich Act was between 37 and 40 percent; the average of the Underwood-Simmons Act was about 27 percent. In order to offset a decrease in customs receipts, the Underwood-Simmons Bill provided an income tax to yield about $100 million in revenue under terms drawn up by Representative Cordell Hull of Tennessee. It was the first income tax under the Sixteenth Amendment, ratified only two months earlier. It imposed a so-called normal tax of 1 percent on personal and corporate incomes over $4,000 and an additional surtax of 1 percent on incomes between $20,000 and $50,000, 2 percent on incomes between $50,000 and $100,000, and 3 percent on incomes over $100,000.[50]

The Underwood-Simmons Tariff never had the opportunity to prove the Democratic premise that it would lower the cost of living or for that matter the protectionist prediction of economic disaster. In less than a year after its passage, World War I began and trade disruptions occurred throughout the world.[51]

Shortly after the passage of the Underwood-Simmons Tariff, the political situation in North Dakota underwent a significant transformation. It occurred as a result of the organization in 1915 of the Non-Partisan League, (NPL), an independent political force that would present a new option to the voters of the state. Convinced that neither party would truly speak for the problems faced by the farmers of the state, the League was started under the presumption that independent political action was needed. The organizer was Arthur Townley, a one-time Socialist who had been an organizer in the state for that party but never a doctrinaire member. He was also a farmer who had gone bankrupt and had turned to political activism after having failed at this trade.[52]

Townley believed that the small farmers of North Dakota had failed to achieve any of their political goals because of their unwillingness to speak as a united force. His program did not vary too much from some of the earlier populist platforms--very little new was to arise from this movement. It was a mixture of populism and nondoctrinaire socialism, and control of some of the small journals within the state which spread their message to the farmers, who rarely read the more conservative papers that were published in the large cities. In 1916 the NPL achieved a remarkable success for a fledgling organization. Backing for the most part insurgent Republicans against regular conservative members of the party, they elected Lynn Frazier as governor, got a majority in the lower house of the state legislature, and barely missed gaining control of the upper house.[53]

The platform, as noted in the previous paragraph, was extremely simplistic. They wanted government ownership of grain elevators, flour mills, packing houses, and storage plants, state inspection of grain and grain dockage facilities, exemption of farm improvements from taxation, state insurance against natural disasters, and rural credit banks operated at cost.[54] They did not speak about the tariff because they did not choose to operate at the national level. They would eventually endorse candidates for the House of Representatives and the Senate, but not without a debate, for, to many of them, issues raised in these bodies were of minimal interest. Eventually, they would change their approach and would become, among other groups in the state, a strong voice on national economic matters and on American entry into the European war.

NOTES

1. George Mowry, *Theodore Roosevelt and the Progressive Movement* (Madison: University of Wisconsin Press, 1946), pp. 46-47; F. W. Taussig, *The Tariff History of the United States* (New York: G. P. Putnam Sons, 1910), p. 363.

2. Ibid., p. 364.

3. Mowry, pp. 46-47.

4. Ibid., p. 47.

5. Ibid; Evans C. Johnson, *Oscar W. Underwood* (Baton Rouge: Louisiana State University, 1980), pp. 124-125; Taussig, pp. 366-367.

6. Mowry, pp. 48-50.

7. Ibid., pp. 50-51.

8. Ibid., p. 52.

9. Ibid., pp. 53-54.

10. Ibid., pp. 54-56.

11. Ibid., pp. 58-59.

12. Ibid., p. 63; Taussig, pp. 395-396.

13. Ibid., pp. 403-404; Mowry, p.64.

14. Johnson, pp. 126 and 134.

15. W. W. Phillips "Asle J. Gronna: Self Made Man of the Plains," Ph.D. thesis, University of Missouri, pp. 205-206.

16. Claude Bowers, *William Beveridge and the Progressive Era* (Boston: Houghton, 1932), p. 365; *Congressional Record*, July 8, 1909 (61st Congress).

17. Donald Anderson, *William Howard Taft, A Conservative's Conception of the Presidency* (Ithaca, N.Y.: Cornell University Press, 1966), p. 36.

18. L. Ethan Ellis, *Reciprocity, 1911: A Study in Canadian American Relations* (New Haven, Conn.: Yale University Press, 1939), pp. 20-27.

19. Bruce Hutchison, *The Incredible Canadian* (New York and Toronto: Longman Greens, 1953), p. 32.

20. James H. Gray, *R. B. Bennett:The Calgary Years* (Toronto: University of Toronto Press, 1991), pp. 117-119.

21. Ruth Warner Towne, *Senator William J. Stone and the Politics of Compromise* (Port Washington, N.Y.: Kennikat, 1979), pp. 91-93.

22. Ellis, p. 108.

23. Ibid., pp. 105 and 120-124.

24. Ibid., pp. 101-108.

25. Ibid., p. 103.

26. Ibid., p. 103.

27. Phillips, pp. 338 et seq.; Richard Norman, "The Election of 1912 and the Progressive Party of North Dakota," M.A., University of North Dakota, 1950, pp. 136-138.

28. Bruce Larson, *Lindbergh of Minnesota* (New York: Harcourt, Brace, Jovanovich, 1971), p. 105.

29. Anderson, p. 139.

30. Ellis, p. 120.

31. Ibid., pp. 120-126; Belle and Fola LaFollette, *Robert M. LaFollette, June 14, 1855-June 18, 1925* (New York: Macmillan, 1953), vol. 1, p. 339.

32. Ellis, pp. 127-128.

33. Ibid., p. 131.

34. Robert Shull, *Laurier: The First Canadian* (New York and Toronto: Macmillan, 1965), pp. 523-533; Kenneth McNaught, *The Penguin History of Canada* (Middlesex: Penguin Books, 1969), pp. 199-202.

35. Elwyn Robinson, *History of North Dakota* (Lincoln: University of Nebraska Press, 1966), pp. 268-269. See also Norman, pp. 56-69.

36. Norman, pp. 135-138.

37. Robinson, pp. 269 et seq.

38. Ibid.

39. Arthur S. Link, *Wilson: The New Freedom* (Princeton, N.J.: Princeton University Press, 1956), pp. 177-178.

40. Ibid., p. 178.

41. Ibid., p.179; *New York Times*, January 1 and 2, 1913, p. 1.

42. Link, pp. 178-179; *New York Times*, November 30, 1912 and January 1 and 2, 1913.

43. *Congressional Record*, April 23, 1913 (63rd Congress).

44. *New York Times*, April 23, 1913; Link, p. 181.

45. Ibid., pp. 183-184.

46. *New York Times*, May 27, 1913.

47. Link, pp. 187-190; *Congressional Record*, May 1927, 1913 (63rd Congress).

48. Link, p. 190.

49. Frank Taussig, "Tariff Act of 1913," *Quarterly Journal of Economics*, 28 (1913): 1-30; Link, pp. 182-191; Johnson, p. 204; *New York Times*, September 10, 1913; *Congressional Record*, September 9, 1913 (63rd Congress).

50. Ibid.

51. Link, p. 196.

52. H. C. Peterson and Gilbert Fite, *Opponents of War: 1917-1918* (Madison: University of Wisconsin Press, 1957), pp. 64-69.

53. Russell Nye, *Midwestern Progressive Politics* (East Lansing: Michigan State University Press, 1959), p. 291.

54. Lewis Crawford, *A History of North Dakota* (Chicago: American Historical Society, 1931), vol. 1, p. 421.

3

World War I

Much of Porter McCumber's efforts in the middle period of his Senate career, 1914-1920, focused on foreign policy. His views on U.S. involvement in the First World War and on the country's entry into the League of Nations have elicited more interest than have his views on economic matters, primarily because historians have been intrigued by the apparent uniqueness of the attitudes of a conservative Republican senator from an isolationist midwestern state.

As Wayne Cole remarks in his biography of Gerald Nye, North Dakota is the most isolationist state in the United States--or at least it was in McCumber's time. The majority of its citizens, particularly those of Scandinavian or German origins, had strong isolationist sympathies.[1] Also prevalent was strong anti-British sentiment, as reflected by Hansbrough's attitude during the Venezuelan Boundary dispute. During the first years of the Great War, North Dakota newspapers almost unanimously urged the United States to stay out of the war and to avoid any semblance of partiality. This antiwar sentiment appeared to cut across all segments of North Dakota politics, ranging from the conservatives as symbolized by McCumber, progressives as represented by Gronna and Helgesen, and the embryonic Non-Partisan League.[2]

North Dakota was not strictly and dogmatically isolationist, however. It supported Cuban intervention in 1898,[3] and it would appear to have supported McCumber in a number of the positions he had taken on international issues up to the point of the First World War. As a strong advocate of international arbitration of disputes, the senator voted in favor of all arbitration treaties, terming them a landmark in achieving

world peace. He regularly voted against any amendments proposed by
nationalist senators to weaken the agreements,[4] and he supported the first
Hague International Conference in 1899 as well as the second in 1907.[5]
He was not impressed, he told his colleagues, with the argument that
some of the provisions might impinge on senatorial prerogatives.[6]
During debates on foreign policy, he repeatedly asserted that the
establishment of peace was more important than narrow parochial
concerns.[7]

On the matter of the United States playing an aggressive role in the
international arena, however, McCumber would shift position from
advocate of arbitration to fervent nationalist. He backed the intervention
in Morocco in 1905.[8] He supported the proposal to send the fleet to
Mexico in 1914 after the altercation with the government of General
Victoriano Huerta, telling the Senate that firmness earlier in the dispute
would have prevented the president from considering this alternative.
However, he was less belligerent after the American forces had landed
in Mexico, stating that the policy was an invitation to war. He
contended that by now the response was excessive for the incident that
had provoked it--the arrest of a few sailors by the Mexican government.
Grounds for wholesale intervention existed, he argued, but not in this
situation. He got into a rather heated debate with John Sharp Williams
of Mississippi who took exception to his remarks that the Mexican
government's refusal to salute the flag was not a good reason for flexing
American military muscle.[9] He told the Senate that if the United States
tried to force out the military leader, Huerta, it would be aligning itself
with what he regarded as an even more unfortunate alternative, Pancho
Villa.[10] Villa would remain a villain to him, and two years later
McCumber would urge that the United States hunt down these
"murdering bandits."[11]

McCumber also reflected the nationalist position on the question of
Philippine independence. He favored giving the Filipinos independence,
for he felt the United States was morally bound to do so. But he was
concerned about a potential military threat to the islands, and he wanted
any instrument of independence to be accompanied by an agreement from
other countries that they would refrain from taking advantage of an
American departure.[12] He believed that the United States could be relied
on to ensure that the Philippines would evolve as a democratic country.
Although he did not fear any loss of their commercial value, he was
concerned that some other European power would move in.[13]

McCumber was one of the few Republicans, however, to support
Wilson when the president proposed repealing the Panama Canal tolls.
On April 6, 1914, he made a speech in the Senate in which he asked his
colleagues: "Will we hide behind the American flag while we burglarize
the treasury to benefit coastwise shipping interest?" He argued that the

United States had to make good on its pledge in the Hay-Pauncefote agreement, and he embarrassed his fellow Republicans by bringing into the debate a statement by one of its leaders, former ambassador Joseph Choate who had been one of the negotiators. Choate had stated that the principle of the treaty was to treat all nations, including the United States, alike.[14]

McCumber spoke on other issues pertaining to foreign policy, although his most prominent addresses were on the subject of intervention in the European war and on the League of Nations. There is little or no evidence that his views provoked any significant opposition within the state. Neither, however, did Gronna; his junior colleague was frequently on the other side of the fence from him on these issues. We might therefore be tempted to suggest that Gronna was defeated as a result of his foreign policy stands in 1920. In truth, however, Gronna fell as a result of political infighting in North Dakota, and not for any public position he took.

McCumber's support for international arbitration and his endorsement of the Hague treaties could serve as a signal that upon the outbreak of the Great War in 1914, he would initially urge that the issue be resolved through diplomacy. Even as the slow "dance of death" that plunged most of Europe into the conflict progressed through the summer of 1914, he was urging mediation. He favored the use of the good offices of the United States to resolve the war.[15] In August 1914, with the German army rampaging through Belgium, he introduced a resolution that called for the United States to be the mediator, a call echoing Wilson's proposal of an earlier time.[16]

McCumber was leery about early efforts to put the United States on a war footing. As late as 1916, he was critical of the interventionist agitation that he contended was an effort to excite the people to demand a military and naval program that would ultimately resemble the armed force of Europe. He argued that large armies and navies would create what he called an "artificial aristocracy" and would control freedom.[17] This position would begin to change, so that ultimately his record on the subject of preparedness would best be described as "mixed."

Although it was not a major concern, McCumber did indicate that he supported an embargo on munitions as a means of keeping the United States from obtaining too great a financial interest in the war. There was only one vote on this matter, and it came at a time when the issue was so presented as to cause confusion about who favored what. The vote was on an amendment to the Ship Purchase Bill of 1915 introduced by Senator Gilbert Hitchcock. The Nebraskan had called for an embargo on munitions almost as soon as it became apparent that the incident at Sarajevo would provoke a major war, and not just another small Balkan brushfire conflict. However, his bad relations with William Jennings Bryan, who privately favored embargoing munitions, and the new chairman of the Foreign Relations Committee, William Joel Stone, prevented a direct vote on the issue.

Hitchcock had to bide his time. His opportunity finally came when opposition developed to a February, 1915 proposal by the administration that it seize the vessels of belligerent countries which were lying in American ports. Hitchcock and a few other Democrats, including the rabidly anti-British James O'Gorman of New York and some others with whom Wilson had patronage difficulties, opposed the measure. The Republican leadership also opposed it, labeling it "socialistic," a sentiment that McCumber echoed. The bill would obviously die, but Hitchcock seeing a chance to use it as a means to test the embargo sentiment in the country, introduced an amendment to the bill which was a copy of his earlier resolution. This further complicated an already confused situation, and the vote must be examined in light of an even more complicating feature; it came on a motion to table, so that supporters of the embargo who would include McCumber voted in the negative.[18] Some scholars, however, cite the lineup as a reasonable definition of who favored an embargo and who did not.[19]

The tabling amendment failed, and eventually the controversial Ship Purchase Bill was also killed. The embargo issue would be raised later, in 1916, in the form of a resolution. McCumber did not speak on its behalf.[20]

McCumber cautioned moderation in formulating the American response to the sinking of the *Lusitania*.[21] Loss of the 128 American lives precipitated a major debate in the United States over the question of what specific action should be taken in light of the sinking, and what long-range position the country should take with respect to unrestricted submarine warfare. The North Dakotan's call for calm and moderation was somewhat counterbalanced by his remarks that in the future unarmed passenger vessels should be allowed to discharge passengers before the submarines fired their torpedoes--in effect neutralizing the effect of unrestricted German submarine warfare.[22] He seemed satisfied by the temporary truce achieved by the *Sussex* Pledge, in which Germany agreed to restrain from unrestricted submarine warfare.

The question of the *Lusitania* and the future of German submarine warfare continued to intrude into the political situation in Washington. The neutralist elements in Congress continued to press for a policy statement from the administration that would indicate its desire for Americans to stay off the vessels of belligerent countries, lest another sinking such as that of the *Lusitania* provoke a louder cry for war. In late February, 1916 Congressman Jeff McLemore, a Bryanite congressman from Texas and Senator Thomas Gore, the blind lawmaker from Oklahoma, introduced a resolution to prohibit American citizens from sailing on these vessels. (Bryan had resigned as Secretary of State over the quality of the official notes on the *Lusitania*). The issue of keeping Americans off the potential targets of war was one aspect of a new problem that now faced President Wilson; the other was a direct challenge to his position that the conduct of foreign policy was the exclusive province of the executive branch. The president managed to mollify a number of antiwar leaders in the Senate such as Stone and Claude Kitchin, the congressional leader from North Carolina who was also a prominent figure in the neutralist bloc.

Stone, Kitchin, and House Speaker Champ Clark then worked to head off agitation for the Gore-McLemore Resolution, aided by a letter from the president to Stone that he would do everything within his power to keep the United States out of war. The statement would appear to conflict with a comment Wilson allegedly made to Stone, the aged lawmaker from Missouri, which indicated that war might not be "a bad idea." Stone repeated this remark to Gore causing a major commotion when the Oklahoman made the statement to this effect on the floor of the Senate. At this point, Stone denied that it was ever made, but the charge further complicated the debate over the resolution.

McCumber clearly favored the Gore-McLemore principle but the parliamentary wrangling that accompanied the debate leaves the position of many other senators in doubt. He tried to introduce his own version of the resolution, one that differed slightly from the original, but it was lost when a Wilson loyalist, moved to table the initial motion--which had been altered to some degree by its author, who then actually voted to table his own motion. Only thirteen senators most of them from the Republican progressive bloc, joined McCumber in voting against tabling. A number of senators complained that the changes in wording and the parliamentary maneuvering prevented a real vote on the merits of the issue.

After the Gore-McLemore proposal faded into history, McCumber took to the floor to explain his position. He claimed that he stood by the principles of international law. Specifically, he stated that citizens of the United States had the right to sail on the vessels of belligerent states and expect that their neutral status would protect them. However, they ought not to take advantage of this right because of the fact that possible deaths would inflame public opinion. In short, it was a right, but one that would have to be surrendered for the duration of the war. In as much as Gore-McLemore--had it become law-- would have suspended what McCumber regarded as a right, his position in supporting the resolution, given his explanation, is less than convincing.[23]

In the immediate aftermath of the debate over Gore-McLemore, McCumber made a statement, which John Cooper believes was one of the first cracks in the seemingly solid bloc of isolationist midwestern legislators. He called for a compact among all nations which would prescribe the rights, duties, and obligations of nations and would create a court to enforce the rules. This is not as much of a reversal as Cooper suggests, however. As has been noted, in the years before isolationism versus interventionism became a major political battle in the United States, McCumber had strongly advocated settling disputes through the Hague Court and he had urged the institution of panels to resolve international problems. As also noted previously, at that time, McCumber had remarked that the surrender of a little bit of sovereignty was a more than justifiable sacrifice in the name of world order.[24]

McCumber was beginning to shift on the subject of preparedness--but perhaps "shift" is not the best word. His early remarks would suggest that he was a strong antipreparedness figure; a more appropriate interpretation would seem to indicate that his was more of a rhetorical than a substantive opposition to preparedness . While he was talking in March, 1916 about "press generated sentiment" for war and likening the proposed American creation of large armies and navies to those of the old world,[25] he was supporting most efforts to do exactly what he seemed to be arguing against. He supported the military buildup and the proposal enlarging the size of the navy. He seemed more concerned about giving President Wilson too much power than he was by calls for the increased size of the armed forces, which he regularly supported.[26] He also went farther than did many strong preparedness advocates by urging compulsory military training in high schools and colleges.[27]

McCumber made his remarks in the spring of 1916 against the backdrop of his 1916 campaign for renomination. North Dakota was an antiwar state, and antiwar rhetoric would help in a state with a strong desire to stay aloof from the conflict in Europe. The Non-Partisan League, now a major factor in the state, was gearing up for a major effort, combining a plea for agrarian reform with a demand for a policy of strict neutralism.

McCumber's only opposition in the primary was Louis Hanna, the former governor, who had been the only political figure of any note to sail on Henry Ford's Peace Ship. Not that Hanna was a strong neutralist; he actually mirrored the incumbent's views on preparedness. Hanna had been born in Pennsylvania and moved to North Dakota early in his life, serving in a variety of government positions before becoming governor in 1912. He had become governor in that year primarily because John Burke chose not to run and the political situation was confused by the presence of three presidential candidates. Hanna initially supported Theodore Roosevelt in the primaries but deserted him for the "regular" Republican in the general election.

The League took a neutral position on the race. This fact aided McCumber because, had they gone with the candidate closest to their positions, they would have endorsed Hanna. McCumber's record on both farm issues and the peace issue made him more attractive to those voters who might otherwise have automatically supported a League endorsed nominee. Hanna's record as governor was credible, but it had been rather mediocre, compared with the record achieved by the dynamic and widely admired Burke. The result was a solid victory for McCumber.

The victory was not as widely celebrated in the McCumber camp as it might have been. John Burke announced that he was returning from Washington to seek the Senate seat. This would prove a more difficult problem for the senior senator who had never run before on a statewide basis, whereas Burke had. McCumber did not have a presidential candidate running in the state stressing the need to stay out of war as Burke had. And there was the problem of the Non-Partisan League, many of whose adherents had voted for the first Democrat ever to hold the governor's chair.

McCumber defeated Burke in the general election, while Wilson, for whom the former governor spent much time campaigning, took the state from Charles Evans Hughes. The margin was small, but it was enough to give McCumber his fourth term in the Senate, the only one he gained by direct election. Part of the legend of North Dakota politics is that McCumber was aided by the unlikely alliance of Alexander McKenzie and Arthur Townley. McKenzie is alleged to have given Townley and his aides money not to endorse and to work for Burke or to have given them assistance in some of their organizational problems. Regardless of the reason, the Non-Partisan League sat on its hands during the campaign and did not help Burke.[28]

The election of 1916 showed that antiwar sentiment was still strong in North Dakota. Ultimately, most elements, save for the Non-Partisan League would come around to the support of the president. Asle Gronna would remain steadfastly antiwar right through the vote in April, 1917; he would be one of only six senators to vote against the war resolution. By the fall of 1916, McCumber had clearly shifted to a point where any pretense of neutralism was gone.

In the fall of that year, following his narrow victory, Wilson was preparing a note that would attempt to oblige both sides in the conflict to declare the terms under which they would be willing to stop the war. At the time Germany had undertaken two different courses of action. It resolved to resume unrestricted submarine warfare, while at the same time suggesting a peace conference. Since Wilson's note came a few days after the German proposal, it was widely misunderstood. McCumber, who was extremely suspicious of the Central Powers' offer,[29] expressed opposition to the president's gambit. A week later, he was even more critical of the chief executive's approach. He would not be a party to placing obstacles in his way, he said, but the president should have let the congress and the public know of his intent. Wilson's timing was bad; it made it appear that his offer implying American participation, was in response to the German note.[30]

McCumber would not endorse the motion which Hitchcock, previously one of the most adamant antiwar figures within the president's party, introduced in the aftermath of the release of Wilson's offer. The resolution would have endorsed all aspects of the president's proposal. However, it immediately ran into the buzzsaw of partisan politics. Republican conservatives, led by Lodge, came out strongly against it, partially because it seemed to imply perpetual American involvement. Hitchcock had introduced the motion without presidential approval, and Foreign Relations Chairman Stone, faithful to Wilson, had to contend with a number of Democrats who were hesitant about it as well.

The resolution was eventually watered down, and finally the proposal that was voted on was one introduced by Republican Wesley Jones of Washington. It managed to get most of the Democratic votes as well as those of most of the remaining antiwar Republicans such as LaFollette, Norris, and Gronna--but not that of Porter J. McCumber. The senior senator from North Dakota sided with his more conservative colleagues on this issue.[31]

McCumber was also critical of Wilson's "Peace Without Victory" speech in January, 1917. Some days later he noted that he agreed that the U.S. should play a part in a world-enforced peace, but that the president's message was much too simplistic. Only a few of the Republican antiwar faction, men such as LaFollette, who called it "an important hour in the history of the world," were supportive. Many others joined Lodge and Borah in worrying about Wilson's references to a League of Nations that might emerge in a postwar world as a vehicle for enforcing this peace--a prospect that McCumber said he did not fear.[32]

Germany had already planned its next move: the formal announcement of its intent to resume unrestricted submarine warfare, announced on January 31 by a note handed by German ambassador Johann von Bernstorff to Secretary of State Robert Lansing. McCumber's immediate response was one of anger. Referring to the *Sussex* Pledge of 1916, McCumber stated that the United States had to show that it would stand by its earlier statements.[33] The following day, he elaborated, urging that all other items be set aside while the Congress deal with this momentous issue. The German note, he observed, could usher in a new era of slaughter and devastation.[34]

McCumber was obviously not alone among the senators in rushing to capitalize on the sentiment sweeping the country in the aftermath of the German note. But there was one aspect of his comment which was absent from most of those by his colleagues. He had not yet abandoned his belief in the rule of law--enforced by a compact of nations drawn together in the mutual belief that this was the only way to resolve differences. Porter McCumber, together with men such as Hitchcock, James Reed of Missouri, Ashurst, and others had abandoned the neutralist position, but only he and the idealistic Hitchcock had the vision to see that the issue extended beyond the current conflict. Both of them would be among the few American politicians talking about an association to enforce the peace after the present conflict ended.

McCumber spoke in favor of a resolution that endorsed the president's actions in breaking diplomatic relations with Germany. Although a resolution was unnecessary, Chairman Stone, on his own initiative, had offered one. Only LaFollette, Gronna, and a few other diehards voted against it.[35]

The senior senator from North Dakota did not stop with his denunciation of Germany's action and his endorsement of the severing of diplomatic relations. He was concerned about the submarines--and for quite some time he would harp on the menace presented by unrestricted submarine warfare. He contended that the use of the submarine violated the most sacred canons of international rules of warfare. He did not even want the Allies to use submarines as part of their own blockade and was concerned that the United States seemed to be retreating from this position. Accordingly, he asked Secretary of State Lansing to clarify the country's position.[36] Two days later, he was at again, critical of Lansing, this time for what he believed was the United States' retreat from its position taken on the *Sussex* Pledge. He did not believe that the United States should simply be waiting for an "overt act" before going further.   To him, it was a retreat from a position of support for international law.[37]

The next flashpoint in the road leading from peace to war was the debate over the publication of the Zimmermann telegram.[38] This now famous communication was sent by Germany to Mexico (over U.S. wires) and intercepted by Great Britain, which held it until a propitious moment arrived. The note held out the promise for Mexico that, should war break out between the United States and Germany, Mexican assistance to Germany might result in the reclaiming of lands once held by Mexico but now part of the United States. The message also suggested that Mexico communicate the nature of this situation with Japan.

The British had intercepted the note as far back as January 16 and had released it to the United States on February 24, two days before the president appeared before the Congress to ask for its endorsement of his proposal to arm merchant ships. This proposal ran into a snag in the Senate Foreign Relations Committee as four senators, including Stone, Hitchcock, and O'Gorman, insisted on an amendment that would prevent the arming of merchant vessels that were carrying instruments of war. Hitchcock would eventually abandon this position.

McCumber supported the proposal as Wilson had originally

presented it. Initially, there had been criticism from the Republican leadership, with several of them expressing worry that Wilson was in the process of acquiring too much power. However, it would have been unwise for a party that had criticized the president for timidity many times in the previous months to refuse him his request, even if, as one put it, it was a bid for autocratic power.

The news that Germany had made such an offer to two countries with whom the United States did not have the best of relations hit Washington with great force. Virtually every lawmaker, including McCumber, rushed to the press with a denunciation of the note. It certainly had one significant effect: with this piece of intelligence available, any opposition to the Armed Ship Bill would now be difficult to explain to the country. Only the hard-core neutralists remained in opposition, determined already to take advantage of the imminent close of the session to filibuster it to death if necessary.

Lodge introduced a resolution asking the president to verify the news stories of March 1, for the note had been "leaked" rather than presented officially. The matter was referred to the Foreign Relations Committee where McCumber joined all but two of the members in supporting the resolution. Stone and O'Gorman were hesitant; they wanted Wilson to reveal his sources, a matter that virtually everyone knew he did not wish to do. Eventually, the resolution, with Hitchcock in charge now that Stone wanted more details, reached the floor where it was subjected to more parliamentary wrangling before finally passing in a way that Wilson could verify its authenticity without revealing sources.[39]

McCumber apparently had no doubts about the authenticity of the note and no concerns over the source of the information. Although anti-British feeling was strong in some parts of North Dakota, it had not affected him to the point where he saw the hand of "perfidious Albion." In fact, Senator Hiram Johnson of California, during the course of the debate over the Treaty of Versailles, would call McCumber one of the "four senators from England".[40]

The Senate Foreign Relations Committee met on February 26 and 27 to discuss the bill, as newspaper reports suggested that any senator who might hesitate to give the president what he wanted would be out of step with the country. The *Bismarck Tribune* was one of those journals that clearly supported giving the president the powers he desired.[41] Eventually, the committee cleared the bill with now only Stone and O'Gorman in opposition, and it even added a clause that strengthened the president's hand. Lodge, the ranking Republican on the committee, had persuaded them to amend the proposal to deal with an 1819 statute which, interpreted strictly, might have placed American ships that fired on German U-Boats in a ticklish international situation.[42]

McCumber supported the bill, but he had what he thought was a more appropriate approach to the problem. Fearful of too great an allocation of power to the president, a point that most Republicans abandoned even before the disclosure of the Zimmermann telegram, he wanted to see the Congress adopt a resolution that would recognize the right of merchant vessels to sail into hazardous waters and the right of these ships to be armed. However, as McCumber would say when he spoke on the floor, he would support the measure that emerged from the Senate Foreign Relations Committee if no one found the substitute preferable. Once again, he was being both legalistic and cautious in his approach to the issue, while remaining well within the boundaries of public opinion. At the same time, Gronna was lining up firmly in the opposition to the bill and was becoming part of the famous Armed Ship Filibuster that would prevent the Senate from voting on the matter before Congress adjourned.

McCumber was clearly opposed to the Stone Amendment, which never came to a vote. A similar amendment was introduced in the House and was voted down, although 124 congressmen, most of them from the Midwest and South voted for it.

McCumber spoke for the Armed Ship Bill on March 2, taking up a great deal of time by stating that he would have preferred the resolution he had introduced.[43] The fact that he spoke for a great length of time could lead us to conclude the he was one of those senators who secretly disagreed with the bill and who promised George Norris, floor manager for the filibusterers, that they would help out by taking a lot of time off the clock by speaking on behalf of the matter. Norris never revealed who these people were, even though his autobiography, written in the 1940s, could have done so without hurting anyone, since by that time most of the Senate of the 64th Congress was dead.[44] However, it would have been out of character for McCumber to have been part of this plan. He signed a "round robin" letter that supporters of the measure circulated, and he signed it without reservations as some of his colleagues did. The "round robin" stated that there was overwhelming support for the proposal to arm merchant ships and that the matter would pass easily if only the filibusterers would allow it to come to a vote. Those senators who did not sign the "round robin" earned for themselves the obloquy of the "The Little Group of Willful Men" and the condemnation of most of the country. Whatever he was, Porter McCumber was not a hypocrite and would not have signed the letter if he had been in favor of the filibuster. The fact that he spoke for a great deal of time (as did others favoring the bill) can be attributed to the fact that he always took more time, even for senators of that period, than necessary to explain his position.

McCumber's speech on the floor, when reduced to its major theme, was little more than a restatement of his position cited in an earlier paragraph. He also stated that he was concerned that the president had seized too much of the prerogative in foreign policy. But in order to demonstrate to Germany that the United States disapproved of its unrestricted submarine warfare, he would stand behind the president in this matter.[45]

The failure of the Armed Ship Bill did not alter the flow of events. Several days after the filibuster prevented a vote on the Armed Ship Bill, Wilson announced that he had discovered that he had the power to arm merchant vessels without the approval of Congress. Even with the president's "discovery" of this power, the question of waging a program of armed neutrality would not get any sort of workout. Events moved much too fast, and by March 20 Wilson had decided that he would ask the United States Congress for a declaration of war against Germany.[46]

The day before Wilson's cabinet met, and the decision was made for war, McCumber announced that he favored a declaration of war. He had finally abandoned whatever effort he might have been attempting to keep one foot in the neutralist camp, although at the time of his announcement, it is doubtful if anyone considered him to be aligned with Gronna, LaFollette, Norris, et al. His statement was a distillation of some of his previous comments, including his early record as a neutralist. He regretted that he could not adhere to the neutralist course, but concluded that through its actions, Germany had left the United States with no real alternative.[47]

Despite a seemingly firm commitment to vote for a war resolution should one be presented, McCumber would have preferred another means of sending the country into conflict. He proposed what Morrison calls a "tripwire" over which Germany could not step without creating a war.[48] What McCumber wanted to do was to place the onus more clearly and distinctly on the Central Powers for any conflict that might arise. He initially offered this resolution when the Foreign Relations Committee met on April 3, a meeting at which only Stone declined to support the president's call for war. Stone then turned the meeting over to Hitchcock, as the next ranking member. No member of the committee showed any enthusiasm for McCumber's substitute.

The North Dakotan's substitute resolution offered a whole battery of points of international law, emphasizing that Congress would determine whether or not the line had been crossed.[49] When the meeting concluded, he symbolically accompanied Hitchcock and Lodge and the remainder of the committee (minus Stone) to the floor of the Senate where they dramatically asked for immediate consideration of the war resolution. Upon objection from LaFollette, it was required that the matter be held until the following day.[50]

The debate over the war resolution on April 4 contained some verbal pyrotechnics, primarily from some of those who still opposed the

United States going to war. Gronna's speech was short and moving, focusing on the fact that the plain people did not want war and at this point that it would be desirable to stage a national referendum to test just how eager Americans were for the conflict.

When McCumber finally took the floor, he delivered one of the longer speeches of the day. It came late in the debate and probably angered some of the senators who were anxious to get the matter over with. First, he talked about his substitute resolution, explaining that, faced with the option, Germany would probably withdraw its declaration of unrestricted submarine warfare. If it did not and it missed the "deadline," it would then have brought the war on itself. McCumber said that he did not think that the German people understood either this matter or the resolve of the United States.

Although McCumber agreed with Gronna that the American people did not want war, he had come to a different conclusion in this matter from that of his junior colleague. He finished by stating that, if his resolution had failed (and by this point in the debate, he was willing to admit to that probability), he would support the war just as vigorously as those who were ready to vote for the war resolution.

When LaFollette took the floor, he invoked the name of a third North Dakota lawmaker, Henry Helgesen. Helgesen was mortally ill (he would die shortly) and in a letter had told LaFollette of the strong opposition to the war in North Dakota. The Wisconsin senator closed the debate with an impassioned plea against the war, which Senator John Sharp Williams of Mississippi contended would have been better suited for the German Reichstag than for the United States Senate. In the end, only LaFollette, Norris, Gronna, Stone, and two others voted against the war resolution.[51]

At this juncture, who more accurately represented the citizens of North Dakota on the subject of war or peace? Robinson would to argue that Gronna's strong arguments were probably more reflective of the general sentiment than were McCumber's. Robinson cites the strong (20 percent) German population, the emphasis on socialism implicit in the Non-Partisan League, and the suspicion that the principal desire for war came from the industrialist East. He also mentions the statistics of the 1916 election which gave Wilson the state, particularly the strong Democratic vote of the antiwar rural counties. At the same time by early 1917 most of the major papers in the large cities had concluded that German behavior had made war inevitable.

McCumber's general posture of neutralism, abandoned only in the last six months before the outbreak of war, would appear to have immunized him from any possible negative reaction. Of course, another six years would have had to elapse before this hypothesis could be tested, and by that time, the war was no longer a political issue in the state. Furthermore, North Dakotans had moved to prosecute the war with considerable patriotic fervor. Even Governor Frazier, who was strongly opposed to declaring war, proved an effective administrator in marshalling the state's war effort. Finally, the debate over the League of Nations showed that McCumber was far more in touch with the general sentiments of the people of his state than Gronna. This might well have tended to obscure any earlier reservations they must have had about his position on a war declaration.[52]

But perhaps more than anything else, McCumber had managed to keep one foot in each camp. His resolution on the floor of the Senate as they were debating the Armed Ship Bill and the war resolutions were vain efforts, as he well knew. But they could have considerable effect on the citizens of his state who were strongly antiwar.

North Dakota's war record was reflected in McCumber's strong support of most methods proposed for prosecuting the conflict. Almost as soon as the ink was dry on the resolution, McCumber was on the floor of the chamber speaking on a resolution that called for a program of agricultural development to prepare the nation for war. What was needed, he said, was a more diversified program. He contended that most cereals are produced in greater quantity than the demand would dictate. The farmers needed help, and they would be facing even greater problems in harvesting their crops as farmworkers were called into military service. Women, he said with great unhappiness, might have to do the work of men on the farms.[53]

McCumber's concern over the plight of the farmer colored much of his thinking during the war. Even before war had been declared, he had withdrawn support for an embargo by indicating that he did not favor such an action on wheat. In January, 1916 he noted that an embargo on wheat and other foodstuffs grown in America's heartland would be unwise, given the current price of farm labor and farm articles. To impose an embargo on these products would be a form of "class discrimination."

His remarks at this time also displayed the twin concept of fiscal and personal austerity, which were a frequent part of his political makeup. Lamenting the status of the farmer, he attributed the bulk of America's economic ills to the relentless pursuit of pleasure followed by many of his fellow citizens. The high cost of living, he announced, could be traced to the $13 billion spent annually for liquor, tobacco, automobiles, and other forms of amusement.[54]

McCumber's concern for the farmer was most manifest in his efforts to persuade the government to raise the minimum price on wheat. The Agriculture Committee, chaired by Gore of Oklahoma, initially proposed an upward adjustment in the price to $2.50 (far more than the administration would accept), while McCumber wanted the price to go to $2.75. Wheat was scarce, he argued, and if the price did not rise to the level he sought, farmers would be operating at a loss.[55]   The administration vetoed the bill proposed by the Congress, leaving the price at the $2.40 level, thus prompting an angry outburst from McCumber. Wilson erred in vetoing the bill, he charged, because he did not have the correct figures.[56]

The wheat shortage was complicated by speculation in 1917 which had temporarily boosted the price to $3.45 before the Chicago Board of Trade suspended trading.[57]   As a result, at least twice during that summer, McCumber had demanded that speculators and hoarders be subjected to jail sentences.[58]   Eventually, by the summer of 1918, the wheat question was resolved, prices per bushel rose, and contributions from other countries such as India, Australia, and Argentina provided sufficient amounts of the commodity to meet the needs of the Allied Powers.   The Food Control Act, despite the senator's misgivings, had come up with a price per bushel that was satisfactory to the farmers.[59]

McCumber generally supported most of the matters pertaining to the conduct of the war. One of his obsessions early in the conflict was still the matter of the German submarines. Unless the United States resolved this problem, he remarked, not all the production in the world would be sufficient.[60] There was no danger of a food shortage, he added, unless a major disaster hit the crops, but getting it to where it could be used remained a problem. It will be recalled that, during the discussion over preparedness, he pressed Secretary of State Lansing for a declaration about submarines representing an "illegitimate" means of maintaining a blockade.[61]

McCumber did not favor high taxes as a means of raising the money necessary for prosecuting the conflict. He argued that it would destroy the spirits of those making large amounts of money and would be a deterrent to production.[62] He supported the bond issue raising $7 billion to fight the war, as he would most similar proposals. Interestingly most of McCumber's speeches on this subject betray a retreat from the fiscal conservatism that dominated most of his political career. And while he would inveigh against waste and corruption, he did not seem as concerned with applying the same standards to wartime measures that he did to peacetime matters.[63]

McCumber was adamant that all Americans do their part. His own son was in the military, and he insisted that there could be no "slacking." He wondered why, even though the United States was involved in a global conflict, productivity seemed to be lower than before. Everyone should be involved in some kind of war work, he contended.[64] He supported the draft[65] and the selective service, and introduced an amendment to the selective service bill that would delete the portion of the measure that exempted conscientious objectors. It was defeated, 54 to 17.[66]

McCumber's support for labor unions, always poor, declined even further during the course of the war. His criticism of strikers was most noticeable in February, 1918, when he urged a crackdown on unions that were not doing their job. He urged that all unions be purged of disloyal "Bolshevik" elements. He hinted that if the country did not move swiftly enough to do so, the events in Russia might be repeated in the United States. He was immediately challenged by two Democratic senators, each of whom responded that labor's record had been excellent.

McCumber replied that his complaints were directed primarily at the International Workers of the World (IWW) and that their record showed disloyalty to the country. He called for a "labor draft" as a means of rooting them out from important positions in the labor movement. Noting the apparent closeness between the government and labor, represented by the important role played in the government by labor's most prominent spokesman, Samuel Gompers, he maintained that labor unions were "slacking" and that the government had surrendered itself to them.[67]

McCumber's remarks on this occasion are interesting for two reasons. That he would attack unions is not surprising, and that he would use the IWW as a club with which to hit all unions suggests a tactic that would become popular with anti-union legislators after the war. McCumber would continue to be critical of labor, condemning the strikes that took place in the immediate aftermath of the peace and joining with others who saw "red" influence everywhere. A second point related to North Dakota politics. To the extent that he had received covert support from the Non-Partisan League in 1916 by its refusal to support Burke, McCumber was certainly burning his bridges to them by such actions. The League had a working relationship with the Agricultural Workers Union which was affiliated with the IWW.[68]

McCumber's concern with Russia and the revolution was not confined to matters of domestic consideration. He was one of those senators who advocated a military presence in that country to counteract communism.[69]

McCumber's record on civil liberties during wartime showed that he was not very scrupulous in caring for the rights of citizens who dissented, although there is little to distinguish him from most of his colleagues. His efforts to force conscientious objectors into the service, a tactic that even most of the more bellicose warhawks rejected, was one manifestation of his belief that, in wartime, pursuit of victory demands unity. On an even more unfortunate level was McCumber's call for President Wilson to remove postmasters who allowed "seditious" material to go through the mails. He wanted them ousted and "patriotic" Americans, who would apparently be willing to serve as censors, put in their place. He warned the president that should he fail to replace the offending officials in North Dakota, the citizens of that state would handle the matter in their own way.[70] This would seem to be in conflict with the climate in his native state, for as Robinson reports, there were relatively few challenges to loyalty and convictions for sedition. He cites future Senator Ladd's observation that North Dakota was an "oasis of sanity in a desert of hysteria."[71]

McCumber was anxious to see the end of the war, but was leery of the initial peace feelers in October, 1918. He joined with Hitchcock and Lodge in expressing reservations about the Central Powers' offer of peace. He wanted the ultimate result of the conflict to represent a German defeat and withdrawal from all territory it had acquired during the war.

One of his most insistent demands was for reparations. In line with his interest in international law, he argued that this was consistent with the situation. Germany must go beyond mere restitution, he maintained, and make reparations to the countries it had attacked. He called for eliminating the German aristocracy, completely disbanding the German army, destroying its arms, and returning all land.[72]

Wilson's reply on the following day did not suit McCumber, who viewed it as incomplete and falling short of complete surrender. When Germany accepted more severe terms several days later and appeared to be giving in on every point, McCumber was less than enthusiastic.[73] He noted that there was one glaring omission. The Fourteen Points that Wilson had proposed as the basis for peace did not mention reparations, and McCumber insisted that they had to be part of any final peace package. However, he did not go so far as to support reprisals, which were being suggested in several quarters, including the corridors and cloakrooms of the Senate. With Hitchcock, he argued that such actions were unnecessary and uncalled for.[74]

NOTES

1. Wayne Cole, *Senator Gerald P. Nye and American Foreign Policy* (Minneapolis: University of Minnesota Press, 1962), pp. 24-25.

2. Elwyn Robinson, *History of North Dakota* (Lincoln: University of Nebraska Press, 1966), pp. 352 et seq. and Paul Morrison, "The Position of Senators from North Dakota on Isolation, 1889-1920," Ph.D. thesis, University of Colorado, 1954, p. 189.

3. Morrison, pp. 90 et seq.

4. Ibid., pp. 136-137 and Herbert Margulies, *The Mild Reservationists and the League of Nations Controversy in the Senate* (Columbia: University of Missouri Press, 1989), pp. 14-15.

5. Margulies, op. cit.

6. Morrison, p. 145.

7. Ibid., pp. 131 and 136-137.

8. Margulies, pp. 14-15 and Morrison, pp. 142-143.

9. *New York Times*, April 15, 1914, p. 2 and April 22, 1914, p. 4.

10. Ibid., April 22, 1914, p. 4.

11. Ibid., March 11, 1916, p. 3.

12. Ibid., January 14, 1916, p. 12.

13. Morrison, pp. 115-119.

14. *New York Times*, April 7, 1914, p. 2. See also Henry Ashurst, *A Many Colored Toga: The Diary of Henry Fountain Ashurst* (Tucson: University of Arizona Press, 1962), p. 31.

15. *New York Times*, August 6, 1914, p. 13.

16. Morrison, p. 184.

17. John Milton Cooper, *The Vanity of Power: American Isolationism and World War I* (Westport, Conn.: Greenwood Press, 1969), pp. 109-110.

18. Thomas Ryley, *A Little Group of Willful Men* (Port Washington, N.Y.: Kennikat, 1975), pp. 42-43.

19. Ibid.

20. Ashurst, pp. 45-46.

21. *New York Times*, May 2, 1915, II, p. 7 and May 15, 1915, p. 5.

22. Morrison, pp. 192-194.

23. Ryley, pp. 47-52 and *New York Times*, March 4, 1916, p. 2. See also Belle and Fola LaFollette, *Robert M. LaFollette, June 14, 1855-June 18, 1925* (New York: Macmillan Co., 1953), Vol. 1, pp. 556-558; Morrison, pp. 204 et seq.

24. Cooper, p. 116.

25. Ibid., pp. 109-110.

26. John Finnegan, *Against the Spectre of the Dragon* (Westport, Conn.: Greenwood Press, 1974), p. 149; *New York Times*, March 18, 1916.

27. *New York Times*, April 7, 1916, p. 1.

28. For information on the 1916 race, see W. W. Phillips, "Asle J. Gronna: Self Made Man of the Plains," Ph.D. thesis, University of Missouri Press, 1958, pp. 437-644; Robert Morlan, *Political Prairie Fire: The Non-Partisan League* (Minneapolis: University of Minnesota Press, 1955), pp. 86-87; Robinson, pp. 355-356 and *New York Times*, June 30, 1916, p. 4. This was the first time that the Seventeenth Amendment, mandating direct election of senators, applied to North Dakota.

29. *New York Times*, December 13, 1916, p. 2.

30. Ibid., December 22, 1916, p. 4.

31. Ryley, pp. 57-58.

32. Cooper, pp. 156-157. Ryley, pp. 57-58.

33. *New York Times*, February 1, 1917, p. 2.

34. Ibid., February 2, 1917, p. 2.

35. Morrison, pp. 221-224.

36. *New York Times*, February 9, 1917, p. 5.

37. Ibid., February 11, 1917, p. 3.

38. For a full account of this incident, see Barbara Tuchman, *The Zimmermann Telegram* (New York: Macmillan, 1966).

39. Material on the floor debate can be found in the *New York Times*, March 2, 1917. For other information, see Tuchman, pp. 160-168 and Ryley, pp. 83-92.

40. Margulies, p. 15.

41. *New York Times*, February 27, 1917, p. 4.

42. Ryley, pp. 79-81; *New York Times*, February 28, 1917, pp. 1 and 3;

43.Ibid, March 3, pp. 1-3.

44. George Norris, *Fighting Liberal* (New York: Macmillan, 1945), p. 178.

45. Ryley, p. 102.

46. Arthur Link, *Woodrow Wilson and the Progressive Era* (New York: Harper and Row, 1954), pp. 274-276.

47. *New York Times*, March 20, 1917, p. 2.

48. Morrison, pp. 238-241.

49. Ryley, pp. 158-162.

50. *New York Times*, April 4, 1917, p. 1.

51. *New York Times*, April 5, 1917, pp. 1-2.

52. Robinson, pp. 355-364.

53. *New York Times*, April 7, 1917, p. 13.

54. Ibid., January 19, 1916, p. 6.

55. Ibid., February 14, 1918, p. 6 and March 17, 1918, I, p. 14.

56. Ibid., July 14, 1918, p. 16.

57. Robert Ferrell, *Woodrow Wilson and World War I, 1917-1920* (New York: Harper and Row, 1985), p. 96.

58. *New York Times*, May 3, 1917, p. 3 and June 2, 1917, p. 2.

59. Ferrell, p. 96.

60. *New York Times*, May 3, 1917, p. 5.

61. Ibid., February 9, 1917, p. 5.

62. David Thelen, *Robert LaFollette and the Insurgent Spirit* (Boston: Little, Brown, 1976), p. 138.
138.

63. *New York Times*, April 18, 1917, p. 4.

64. Morrison, p. 245. See also *New York Times*, February 1, 1918, p. 18.

65. *New York Times*, May 28, 1917, p. 2.
66. Ibid., May 2, 1917, p. 3.
67. Ibid., February 26, 1918, p. 7.
68. Robinson, p. 369.
69. *New York Times*, February 20, 1919, p. 11.
70. Ibid., July 24, 1917, p. 24.
71. Robinson, p. 367.
72. *New York Times*, October 8, 1918, pp. 1 and 5. See also Morrison, pp. 245 and 250.
73. Ibid., October 9, 1918, p. 1.
74. Ibid., October 13, 1918, p. 3.

4

The League of Nations

Many historians tend to call Porter McCumber one of the few heroes of the League of Nations fight. He is reputedly one of the few government figures to emerge with any degree of honor from what some consider one of the more dishonorable episodes in American history. At the same time, some element of wonder exists that a conservative Republican from one of the most isolationist states in the country would so strongly advocate a treaty binding the United States to a world body that could involve it in affairs outside its border. Most historians, however, did not really know much about Porter McCumber and took him on face value, choosing not to consider those aspects of his personality that make his commitment to the Versailles Treaty and to the League much more understandable.

The question of whether McCumber was a hero is open for doubt. At a key point in the fight over the treaty, McCumber opted for a course of action that only deepened the lines between Wilson and his followers on the one hand and the opponents of the League on the other. Perhaps it was unfair to expect him to rise above partisan politics in a way that few statesmen of the 20th century have been able to do.

The first question about McCumber and his commitment to the treaty and League of Nations evolves around the character of North Dakota. Here we must take into account the role played in the second decade of the 20th century by the Non-Partisan League in the state. This movement was becoming more powerful during the period between 1916 and 1920, winning a number of seats in the state legislature for its endorsees. It was also supportive of the idea of a new democratic world order, endorsing more of Wilson's Fourteen Points than did either of the two major parties. It was an internationalist movement at this stage of its development, and its policies called for the participation of the United States in the League. In addition, as Robinson notes, many of the states' newspapers supported the treaty and the legislature twice passed resolutions favoring U.S. membership in the world body.[1]

This is not to suggest that McCumber had adopted the entire platform of the Non-Partisan League. Had he done so, he would not have been defeated in 1922. Rather it is only to indicate that whatever reputation North Dakota had as an isolationist state, the power of the Non-Partisan League and the general support by other groups made it safe for McCumber to support the Versailles Treaty in 1919-1920. McCumber was very much in step with a majority of his constituency. Asle Gronna, who was a member of the "Irreconcilables," twelve Republicans who fought the treaty and eventually succeeded in killing it, may have taken a position more in keeping with the traditional attitude of North Dakotans in world affairs, but he was out of step in this instance.

The traditional portrait painted of the isolationism that marked the United States during the period between the incident at Sarajevo and the end of the 1920s shows that it was strongest in the Midwest, between the farm belt and the Pacific coast. It was most vocal in the rural areas, and especially in places where citizens whose origins were from Germany, Sweden, Norway, and other Scandinavian countries. Certainly, that fits North Dakota, which was a strong anti-interventionist state from 1914 to 1917[2]. McCumber might be regarded as an isolationist because he joined with most of the men who came from the areas described above in urging a policy of neutralism on the United States in the years between 1914 and 1917. Some of these studies fail to consider the difference between isolationist and neutralist, because so many prominent figures, particularly Norris and LaFollette, were both. A number of important figures in American politics who came from the area that opposed involvement in World War I were not isolationists. They were internationalists, who did not oppose American involvement in world affairs but who had reservations about involvement in the European war.

If LaFollette, Norris and Gronna represent one side of the equation, McCumber represents the other--a commitment to internationalism, while at the same time holding reservations about the European war. Also in this category would be his onetime law school classmate, Hitchcock of Nebraska. Even William Jennings Bryan might be placed in this category, although at the time of the debate over the Versailles Treaty, his behavior had become erratic and his support for the League was compromised by some of his other concerns.

Yet another consideration is that McCumber was always perceived, and not always incorrectly, as a faithful party wheelhorse and the

Republican party is identified as the instrument that killed the treaty and the League of Nations. One can debate just how faithful he was to the party; however, the perception that the party was uniformly opposed to the treaty is incorrect. A list of notable Republican leaders who favored American ratification of the Versailles Treaty and entrance into the League would begin with former President William Howard Taft and would include, in varying degrees, many of the distinguished members of the eastern establishment faction of the party. A more detailed examination of divisions within the Senate belongs in another section of this chapter, but for our present purposes, it must be noted that McCumber's support of the League scarcely represents apostasy within the ranks of the party.

Lastly, it needs to be repeated that McCumber's longstanding support for international tribunals and international arbitration agreements should have directed anyone examining the treaty fight to conclude that anything other than support would have been out of character. Of all the senators in the 66th Senate, Porter McCumber's support for the treaty and the League might have been the most predictable, based on past record.

McCumber's stand on the Versailles Treaty and his strong advocacy of an international organization would cause Henry Cabot Lodge to undertake his famous effort to stack the Foreign Relations Committee in the summer of 1919. Now that the elections of 1918 had put the Republicans in control, they and not the Democrats could dictate committee alignments. Lodge knew that McCumber was going to support the president and the treaty. In the spring, he had refused to sign the "round robin," which committed its signatories to oppose what they believed Wilson was going to be bringing back from Paris.[3] Lodge could accept McCumber's opposition, but he could not accept the problem presented by his presence on the Foreign Relations Committee. He needed to place friendly faces on that panel, and that would be no easy chore. This task was made more difficult by the announcement by several Republican progressives that they were going to challenge the naming of some conservatives for some of the powerful committee chairmanships. One of their targets was Boies Penrose, chairman presumptive of the Senate Finance Committee, on which McCumber was then the second-ranking Republican member.

The Republican leader had to be concerned that Senate Democrats might join with dissident Republicans and not only prevent him from stacking the Foreign Relations Committee, but deny the party key chairmanships as well. At one point, Lodge had a conversation on the subject with Gilbert Hitchcock, the acting Democratic leader and ranking member of the Foreign Relations Committee. The Nebraskan would have the task of piloting the treaty Wilson brought back from Paris through the Senate, and he was capable of counting noses, as was the

Massachusetts lawmaker. Hitchcock offered Lodge the commitment that he would not assist the progressives, if the Massachusetts senator would agree to change the allocation of senators on the Foreign Relations Committee from 10-7 to 10-8. If Lodge had agreed, it would have jeopardized his chances of controlling the committee and the hearings into the proposed treaty, so he rejected the matter. Therefore, an agreement to ten Republicans and seven Democrats was reached.

If the figure had gone to 10-8, Lodge might have had serious problems. Since he had already seen McCumber's probable defection on most questions, he could not afford one more accommodating member of the majority party. This could produce a 9-9 split, with McCumber joining what Lodge believed would be a solid phalanx of Democrats in support of the agreement. Had he known that at least one, John Shields of Tennessee, would bolt from the leadership, he might not have been so concerned. But he could take no chances. He rejected the "bait" and took his chances with the deliberations that eventually resulted in Penrose and the others being named by the party caucus and confirmed by the Senate.[4]

Then came the matter of "stacking" the committee. McCumber's seniority ensured him a position, but Lodge wanted to be sure that he remained the only "mild reservationist" on the committee. Therefore, Lodge ignored Frank Kellogg of Minnesota, whose background suggested that he belonged on the committee, William Kenyon of Iowa and others, and placed people in the body who were "strong reservationists" or Irreconcilables. This ensured him control of not only the committee but also of the vote on most issues. Only a few times did any of the Republicans desert to give McCumber and the Democrats an advantage, and most of these occurred on procedural matters.

Some Republicans grumbled in the coatroom about Lodge's tactics in stacking the committee. Democratic critics noted this dissatisfaction in their speeches but did not identify any of them. If McCumber was critical of his leader, that fact is lost to history because he remained a good party man on this issue, leaving the complaining to the Democrats who saw the implications of Lodge's tactics.[5]

Before proceeding with the account of McCumber's role in the treaty fight, we must define the three distinct groups of Republican senators which emerged during the fight for the League. The members of one group are easy to define: the Irreconcilables, as noted earlier, were composed of some twelve Republicans (and one Democrat, James Reed of Missouri) and included Borah, Philander Knox of Pennsylvania, Frank Brandegee of Connecticut, Hiram Johnson of California, Albert Fall of New Mexico, LaFollette, Norris, and Gronna.[6] The other two groups are a little harder to define, as lines shifted on specific parts of the treaty.

The "mild reservationists" were headed by McCumber, who was

the only one of them to sit on the Foreign Relations Committee.   In addition, clearly in this set would be found Charles McNary of Oregon, Kellogg of Minnesota, Knute Nelson of the same state, LeBaron Colt of Rhode Island, and Irvine Lenroot of Wisconsin.   Early in 1919, these senators and a few other like-minded members of the majority party had begun to meet to discuss the question, much of the time under McCumber's direction.

The next group is somewhat amorphous.   They have been called the "strong reservationists" because they preferred major changes in the document.   Its members would range from Henry Cabot Lodge, who was very close to the Irreconcilables and, in some people's minds, a closet member of the group, to another collection who would sit somewhere between the Massachusetts senator and colleagues such as Warren Harding of Ohio and the clearly definable "mild reservationists."   Not all historians agree on just who stood where, and the question is not pertinent to this study.   But one thing can be determined: the presence of McCumber and a handful of others as "mild reservationists," who at least initially willing to look with considerable favor on Wilson's treaty, was a problem for Lodge and the Senate leadership. [7]

Representatives of all sides in the fight viewed McCumber as a key figure.   As the only "mild reservationist" on the Foreign Relations Committee, he appears to have taken the initiative with his moderate colleagues and to have negotiated for them at certain points.   Taft, the most prominent nonsenatorial Republican supporter also dealt with McCumber, albeit through an Ohio newspaperman, Gus Karger, who was Taft's eyes and ears in Washington.[8]   In the final analysis, when Republican lines had to be drawn, it was Lodge who sat down with McCumber to work out the final compromise on the most controversial of the articles, Article X, which would commit the United States to involvement in all League projects, including the dispatching of troops to trouble spots.

Several points were at issue in the treaty fight.   Although it is beyond the province of this book to discuss them all, a brief notation of the more important might be in order.   Many senators were concerned about the status of the Monroe Doctrine, and others were most concerned about "domestic hegemony," which implied the right of the United States (and the several) states to manage their internal affairs without interference from the League.   But Article X and its implications for the United States, should some world problem appear to require involvement by the League and its members, was the most difficult of the problems to resolve.   If nothing else, failure to agree on this issue, which to many observers lay at the heart of the dispute, doomed Wilson's treaty.

The other issues were less important overall, although they had great relevance to some senators.   Hiram Johnson of California insisted on a provision that would prevent Britain from having five votes

(Canada, Australia, etc.).   Even McCumber became a "strong reservationist" with regard to one particular matter--the presence of the United States in the world labor organization (ILO). In view of his fears that Bolshevism might emerge from certain types of unions during the war, this was hardly a surprising position for him to take.

McCumber began his defense of the treaty even before the president's first visit to Paris. That visit would become the focus of early Republican criticism. Some lawmakers even suggested that, should the chief executive leave the country, the office was to be considered vacated. McCumber argued that this was nonsense and that the president should be allowed to proceed. He contended that if the United States truly wanted to end war, procedural matters should not be allowed to interfere with the direction and purpose of the trip.[9] He conferred (along with Lodge, Brandegee, and Borah, all of whom were antagonistic to the president and his purpose) with Henry White, the veteran Republican diplomat whom the chief executive had selected as the "token" member of the now-majority party on the peace commission. This meeting took place before White accepted his role.[10]

McCumber's inclusion in this luncheon meeting is significant. Lodge obviously knew of the North Dakotan's general disposition in the matter as well as the strategic position he occupied. So did other members of the minority, which is no doubt why those pro-League senators who would constitute the "mild reservationists" would look to him for leadership.

McCumber's first major comments on the treaty and the League was presented shortly after the first of the year, while the president was still in Paris. "Must history repeat itself over and over again. Must our children's children suffer and die as their fathers have suffered and died to propitiate the god of war," he told his colleagues. McCumber had little patience with those who contended that there was entirely too much haste in committing the United States to a world organization; he called the idea of an international body an absolute necessity. If we do not capitalize on our victory, he warned his colleagues, we will have fought, and many young men have died, in vain. He scored the various criticisms being voiced against the League--that it created a "super state" that would destroy American hegemony in domestic matters and that it would threaten the existence of the Monroe Doctrine.

McCumber found the idea that the League of Nations would involve the country in a series of entangling alliances to be a foolish one. He noted that many of the senators who used this argument appeared to have had no difficulty in voting for an "entangling alliance" in April, 1917 which put the United States into the war with a whole list of other countries. If we can do it to wage war, he said, why not to wage peace. Perhaps, he hinted, some of these arguments were misplaced and suggested a hidden agenda.   He also objected to the constitutional arguments that were being raised by opponents of the League.[11]

In late February Wilson returned to a growing crescendo of criticism coming from anti-League quarters. The president met with the Senate Foreign Relations Committee and the House Foreign Affairs Committee on February 26 and laid out the issues for them. The responses varied, as did the versions that the senators gave to the press the next day. Democrats such as Hitchcock were favorable, while anti-league or "strong reservationist" Republicans such as Lodge, Brandegee, and Knox were critical.[12]

McCumber's most important reaction to the criticism of Wilson and of his performance at the White House meeting came on March 3, when he replied to the isolationist Senator Lawrence Sherman of Illinois. The North Dakota senator noted that Wilson had to worry about other countries and that most of his critics seemed to forget that. In addition, he remarked, most of the criticisms seemed to be very farfetched. Perhaps the United States would have to go to war in the event the League could not maintain the peace, but even if the United States stayed out of that body, it might still have to go to war in some situations. The time had come, he told his colleagues, to concentrate on the "Grand Purpose" and to stop quibbling over technicalities.

McCumber admitted to some of the criticism being leveled at the document, the first drafts of which were now being circulated. He agreed that some of it was loosely drawn, and he indicated that he did not object to some minor changes. At no point during the debate would he insist on the document being adopted without change, and there would always be some minor changes to which he would agree. On this occasion, however, he said that senators were deliberately reading it out of context. He was adamant in his statement that Wilson had been fair in his presentation, thus contradicting the Republican senatorial leadership.[13]

McCumber condemned the attitude of some of his colleagues, calling upon them to be honest with themselves and with the country. "If we believe that we are in honor and in duty bound, if we do not believe that there is any moral obligation resting upon this great nation to assist in maintaining the peace of the world, then let us at least do what we can to assist other nations in making an agreement that we can all stand by."[14]

While McCumber was speaking, an action that would undercut his efforts to show that there was some Republican sentiment for the League was taking place. Apparently at the instigation of Brandegee, a petition was being circulated among Republican senators which read that they would dissent from any treaty, and most certainly one in the form they believed would emerge from Paris. Lodge read the statement and the names of the petioners to the Senate.

McCumber had declined to sign the statement. Actually, only thirty-seven members of the party signed--enough to ensure a vote against the treaty--but twelve had not. Kellogg, Nelson, Kenyon, and McNary were also among those who did not sign. Norris and LaFollette did not sign, and they, of course, could be relied on to oppose the treaty.[15] LaFollette stated that he did not sign because the "round robin" did not address the important issues as he interpreted them.[16] Gronna's name was on the list.

LaFollette's situation was interesting. Most of what has been described in this chapter had taken place during the "lame duck" session of the 65th Congress; the new 66th Congress would take its place shortly. The Democrats were still technically in control, even though the results of the election in 1918 had given the Republicans a 49-47 majority for the new Congress. During the previous year, Kellogg had charged the fiery Wisconsinite with some "seditious" utterances, based on a statement LaFollette had made while speaking about the war. The Senate was looking into the matter as the war ended, and when the Republicans discovered the results of the elections, they realized that LaFollette's seat was crucial to the organization of the Senate of the 66th Congress. Therefore, they had to defend his seat, even though most members of his party would have preferred to see him retired to private life and probably agreed with the sentiments expressed in the charges. Were he to be ejected and a Democrat elected in his place, the count would be 48-48 and Vice-President Thomas Marshall could break the tie and give the Democrats the right to continue as the majority party in the Senate. That would deny Lodge the role of chairman of the Foreign Relations Committee.[17]   So they voted to dismiss the charges.[18] McCumber joined with his colleagues in defending the Wisconsin senator.

Wilson returned from Paris early in July, 1919 to face a summer of growing tension over the fate of the treaty. In the interim several fights had taken place in Washington over aspects of the League question. Lodge, as previously noted, had "stacked" the Foreign Relations Committee early in June,[19] largely because of his inability to deal in any other way with the problem posed by McCumber.[20] Then there was a resolution presented during the May of that year which would separate the treaty ending the war from consideration of the League.

Early in June, still another firestorm hit the Senate with the revelation that copies of the treaty, which was to be signed shortly in Paris, were circulating in Washington. They were not supposed to be made public, although they were available in foreign capitals and the Republicans were taking considerable political advantage of the situation. How they got to the United States and whether they represented a true picture are a subject for another work. However, their presence could not be ignored. Hitchcock and the Democrats protested that they were stolen goods and Johnson of California demanded that the treaty be read at this time to the Senate. A resolution to that effect was passed, with only

McCumber among the Republicans voting against it. Even some pro-treaty Democrats voted to publish.[21]

McCumber had also joined with Democratic members of the Foreign Relations Committee in opposing a resolution by Philander Knox, the former secretary of state and currently an Irreconcilable. This resolution would separate discussion of the treaty from consideration of the League of Nations. Despite McCumber's defection, the resolution passed the Foreign Relations Committee and the Republicans prepared to push it on the floor. Hitchcock called the move a "grave menace" and said that the Democrats were ready to prevent the matter from coming to a vote. He did not use the word "filibuster" but rather said that there would be "extended debate" on the subject. McCumber apparently conferred with the Nebraskan on the subject, and plans called for him to lead off for the opponents of the Knox resolution. Hitchcock indicated that other Republicans might join the battle. The Republican leadership eventually withdrew it, since it was unnecessary to their ultimate purpose and had been designed more as harassment than as anything else.[22]

Despite McCumber's willingness to work with the Democrats on this issue and other procedural considerations, he and his fellow "mild reservationists" remained aloof from the Democrats on the more substantive questions. Much of this attitude was due to the fact that Hitchcock and the Democratic leadership, acting under instructions from Wilson, were willing to concede nothing at this point by way of changes. It was at this juncture in the treaty fight that Hitchcock and McCumber might have formed a coalition to save the treaty. But Hitchcock was held back by the knowledge that the president would oppose any program that might arise from such a coalition's efforts, and the Democrats had been conditioned to obey their leader. McCumber, who was more willing to negotiate than Hitchcock, had to deal with party considerations of his own. A Wilson victory could have serious implications for the presidential election in 1920.

Hitchcock did try to bring about some agreement through an indirect route. Since he could not persuade the president directly to accept some compromises and work with the "reservationists," he decided to see if these men would change the president's mind. He got Wilson to talk with a number of moderate senators, including the senior senator from North Dakota, and, beginning on July 16, a dozen or so Republican lawmakers went to the White House for individual discussions with the chief executive.[23] McCumber's version of events is very noncommittal. He would only say that the president did not give him too much pressure and had revealed some confidential information to him. He added that he supported the document without reservations but would accept changes as a means of political expediency. Here, no doubt, he was referring to the need to get some of his moderate colleagues to go along.[24]

McCumber also spoke to Taft about the conversation. The former president wrote Hitchcock after having conferred with Karger. Taft urged the acting Democratic leader to abandon an unconditional posture of no reservations and work with moderates such as McCumber.[25]

The treaty then disappeared into the Senate Foreign Relations Committee where Lodge planned a long set of hearings that were designed to draw out the process as much as possible. According to reports, it was this policy which he had promised Borah, the spokesman for the Irreconcilables, who had wanted an all-out attack on the treaty and the League. Lodge hoped to protract the process for an extended period of time. To this end, he and the committee indicated that they would hear anyone who wanted to say anything at all about the document.[26] Hitchcock and the Democrats protested, arguing that the committee's opposition to the president's proposed plan was a foregone conclusion; extending it only delayed the moment when everyone would have to vote on it.[27]

McCumber shared Hitchcock's dismay at the extended process of the hearings. When the Irreconcilables on the committee indicated they wanted testimony from some of those who had been in Paris and were still there, he balked. He and Harding joined the Democrats in restricting testimony by indicating that the committee would not wait to hear them.[28] McCumber was also continuing to meet with at least six of the moderates, including Lenroot, Kellogg, McNary, and Colt. By late July, they had agreed on four reservations, some of which they had discussed with former Secretary of State Elihu Root.[29] Moderates had been conferring with other pro-League Republicans, including Columbia President Nicholas Murray Butler, who had attempted a compromise arrangement, but who had seen his ideas rejected by President Wilson earlier in the summer.[30]

One issue that was becoming a greater problem for the treaty's supporters was one that had nothing to do with the League of Nations. It centered on the award of the Shantung area of China to Japan and had set off a nationalistic fervor among supporters of reservations. They would not consent to it at all. McCumber had no problems with this issue. He denounced the Foreign Relations Committee, which by a 9 to 8 vote had added an amendment rejecting the award. McCumber called it a "poisoned blade."[31]

McCumber said that he wanted to give Japan time to act justly in the matter. Speaking to the Senate on August 26, he indicated that the League of Nations would be China's defense against any further plunder. He thought that it represented a false promise to the fledgling Chinese government, and he contended that should the matter fail, the United States was committing itself to the use of its own troops to drive the Japanese out of Chinese territory. Ultimately, he would vote for a reservation on the subject, but he found the out-and-out provision that

Japan must get out of China objectionable. He went so far as to suggest that the advocates of this provision might be using it as a means of discrediting the entire treaty.[32]

McCumber similarly viewed the efforts to alter the voting patterns so that the former British empire states would not be able to vote on matters pertaining to the mother country. No one else would have signed the treaty in Paris if they believed that Great Britain was going to have six votes, he argued. England, he said, could not control its self-governing dominions in these matters. The amendment, he contended, was destructive. He tried to develop a compromise amendment within the committee but found no support for it.[33]

Article X, the provision that would open the possibility for American involvement in settling world problems with the possible use of troops, was causing the main problem in committee. Many students of the subject suggest that had this issue been resolvable, most of the others would have fallen into line. Republicans insisted on maintaining the prerogatives of the Congress in this matter or wording it in such a way that American involvement would be all but meaningless. McCumber supported the provision as Wilson had brought it home from Paris right from the beginning.[34] However, as this issue became more intense, he joined the effort to develop a compromise that might satisfy both sides. Like most of his other efforts during this period, it was futile.

On August 19, McCumber joined his colleagues from the Senate Foreign Relations Committee at the White House to talk to the man who had been the chief negotiator at Paris. The accounts of the meeting suggest few fireworks and few departures from what we might reasonably have interpreted from the participant's prior behavior. Lodge stayed out of the dialogue as Borah, Brandegee, and Knox conducted most of the questioning, and not always in a friendly tone. Harding bumbled through some of the few comments he was to make. Hitchcock, Williams, and Claude Swanson of Virginia took up the defense when the president needed it. McCumber occasionally stepped into the conversation.

Despite his objections to the way the Republicans were using the Shantung issue, McCumber indicated in the meeting that he doubted Japan would carry through on its commitment. He asked that the president produce the notes of the convention, particularly those on Shantung. He did not understand what was meant by that country returning the province to China "as soon as possible."[35]

McCumber wanted to know about the treaty with France, which would guarantee American support for that country. He could not understand what the president had said in response to an earlier question about this obligation being a legal as opposed to a moral one. As he saw the problem, if it was a legal obligation, the country had a moral obligation to obey it. Wilson agreed that this was a proper interpretation of the matter.[36]   He also asked the president about reparations. He had understood that a commission would have to decide whether the country had a right to them. Wilson responded that this was not the case and that the country would make the determination for itself. Then came the question of whether or not the Congress would be involved in the decision.[37] The chief executive did not know the answer.

McCumber also asked about the right of the United States (or any country) to withdraw from the League. This, too, had become a sticking point for many critics of Wilson's plan.   The language bothered McCumber because once again it seemed to touch on the question of a legal issue versus a moral one. He asked the president if he would accept a reservation clarifying the language so as to indicate that a country could decide for itself when it could begin the process of withdrawing from the League and how it would determine that all of its moral obligations had been met.[38]

These are just a few of the comments and observations McCumber made during the discussion. Clearly he was not unfriendly, and he was anxious that the president understand the need for clarifying reservations (as opposed to the more serious amendments that the Republican majority on the committee was planning). Yet at the same time, the friendship for the treaty and the support for it that he had been proclaiming on the floor and in the committee room were not there. If Wilson or Hitchcock had been counting on a public break with the Republican majority, they had to be disappointed.

McCumber had one last communication with Wilson before the president left on his ill-fated tour of the west--followed by a Republican truth squad that included Borah and Johnson and from which he returned crippled from a stroke. McCumber urged the chief executive to stress the issue of England's relationship to Ireland, the question of dominion voting, and the issue of Shantung. (None of these issues bothered McCumber, but he understood the political problems attached to each.) He advised Wilson to tell the public that the United States would not go to Great Britain's defense in the event of revolt in one of its colonies.[39]

The report of the Senate Foreign Relations Committee came to the full body in early September, 1919.   The main part of the report submitted by Lodge and eight other Republicans, constituted the majority report, replete with both amendments and reservations. Amendments were the more serious of the changes, for they would vitally alter the nature of the document. The reservations meant that the United States joined with serious misgivings. These were equally unacceptable to Wilson, although he had abandoned the concept of no reservations, as long as they did not change the relationship between the United States and the world body. He had told the senators in his August meeting that he did not object to some minor considerations.

The Democrats, except for Shields of Tennessee, who would not sign any report, supported Hitchcock's minority report. The final report was submitted by one man--Porter J. McCumber, who as a minority of one found it necessary to file a document detailing his own views of the situation, regardless of how he had voted on specific matters in committee. In writing his report, he was indicating that he was not in sympathy with the majority document. Nor was he willing to work with the minority headed by Hitchcock who, at the moment, still appeared unwilling to consider even the mildest of reservations. Secretly, the president had agreed to some reservations--changes that he had personally authored and given to the floor leader, noting that he could use them at a propitious moment but with a denial of real authorship. Hitchcock would reword them in a way to make them even more palatable to Congress.[40]

McCumber submitted his report on September 11, after the majority and the minority reports had been presented. It was regrettable, he remarked, that partisanship had been allowed to enter into such a grave matter. He seemed more critical of the majority (the members of his own party) than of the president. He suggested that much of the opposition to the treaty was the result of personal antagonism and that some Republicans seemed to be unaware of the president's prerogatives. He noted that the majority report had not even tried to explain, as was the custom, the purpose of the treaty. They were not ready to indicate any of the good that the proposal might accomplish. McCumber's criticism was extraordinarily harsh and even somewhat sarcastic as he noted that the United States, which had always been supportive of the peaceful resolution of international disputes was now rejecting a proposal made to accomplish peaceful initiatives. For himself, he would be content with a few (six) mild reservations, although he gave no indication as to whether or not other "mild reservationists" might share in this approach.[41]

McCumber's report was praised; phrases such as "high minded" were not uncommon. He had summarized the events and had provided as good a critique of the fight over the treaty as any dispassionate observer might have. He showed that partisanship had colored the debate and that the majority led by Lodge had not even addressed the possible advantages. The effect of his speech was not lost on Lodge. While the Massachusetts senator could defeat the Wilson treaty with or without the North Dakotan, he could not bring about passage of his own version, the one with significant reservations, without McCumber's support and that of other "mild reservationists."

Wilson did not seem to appreciate either the speech or the advice in McCumber's letter of late August. He made two stops in North Dakota during his ill-fated swing through the west, in Mandan and in Bismarck. His intent, of course, was to counter Gronna's opposition to the treaty, but little if any praise for the state's senior senator escaped his lips. Wilson had also made this issue into a partisan one, a point not lost on McCumber. The president's popularity had reached a very low level, as even the normally sympathetic Ashurst remarked. Ashurst also observed Wilson's efforts were producing no converts to the treaty.[42]

Hitchcock's job became even more complex following Wilson's stroke. He could not talk with the stricken leader, and he was facing a challenge to his position as acting minority leader from Underwood and the southern Democrats, some of whom were beginning to desert the treaty. The few efforts he made to talk to McCumber and the other moderates about the question were compromised by his status as well as the president's illness. Thus, with this consideration, McCumber began to move toward the Lodge position. Since he and his fellow moderates could not work with the Democrats, whose position was closer to theirs, they would have to work with the leadership of their party, symbolized by Lodge--who also needed to chart a course that would keep the Irreconcilables from creating troubles that would upset his plans.

Lodge began to draw the moderates into framing compromise language on the reservations that the committee majority had reported out in early September. On September 22, he invited McCumber to lunch so that the two could sit down and work out the language of Article X, the "backbone of the treaty," as Lodge would later call it. They agreed on a wording that each could accept, and, they took it back to their supporters for approval. The Massachusetts senator would later write to a friend that, in getting McCumber to agree to the wording on this matter, "he had travelled a long way."

The language of the new reservation was far stronger than what McCumber had originally called for. When the joint version reached Wilson on September 23, the president reacted violently, declaring that it was a complete betrayal of the covenant. When it reached the floor, it bore McCumber's name, not Lodge's, just as other changes in language reached after discussion with other moderates bore their sponsorship as well. Lodge had effectively moved to shore up one of his flanks and had permanently removed any possibility that the Democrats could exploit this group.[43]

Why had McCumber taken this tack? Clearly, he had destroyed any possibility that he and the other moderates could work with the Democratic leadership, or at least some "rump faction" within the minority party. In his efforts to get the United States into the League of Nations, McCumber, however, had clearly miscalculated Woodrow Wilson. If the treaty had passed with the strong reservations attached (the spirit of Lodge, tied to the sponsorship of McCumber), Wilson would have declined to accept it. McCumber's explanation was that while he still favored milder reservations, Wilson's attitude made it impossible to do otherwise. Faced with siding with Wilson or Lodge, he chose to stand with his Republican colleagues.[44] Perhaps, in fairness, he had no choice.

McCumber continued to confer with Taft, who still clung to the idea that only modest changes were warranted.[45] These conversations suggest that he still felt more at home with the sort of changes that he (and Hitchcock) favored, but that he was betrayed by Wilson's attitude and the Democrats' blind partisanship. But when the Democrats offered a modification of their original Article X, one that virtually squared with the proposal McCumber had made earlier, he declined to accept it.[46] On November 13, he said that, in order to achieve the purposes he sought, it would be necessary to support the strong reservations. He had become a "strong reservationist."

McCumber would go along on Article X and some of the other reservations, but he remained strongly opposed on others. He continued to oppose the reservation on Shantung, and he would not support the effort to curtail voting rights for former British dominions that had gained independence. He had voted against the amendments on these matters and now against the reservations as well. He had also voted against the committee-sponsored preamble providing that the League would go into effect with or without the approval of smaller nations.[47] All committee reservations passed. One reservation was added from the floor, a proposal that McCumber sponsored. He had maintained that the most unacceptable part of the treaty was its labor provision, and he wanted it understood that the United States would not be part of any labor organization unless Congress approved. This proposal was added by a vote of 54 to 35. McCumber again voiced his fears of the IWW in the postwar world. (While a two-thirds vote was necessary to pass the treaty, amendments and reservations needed only a simple majority to be added.)[48]

On November 19, the Senate voted on the treaty with the "Lodge reservations" attached. Prior to the vote, the Democrats had caucused and heard a letter from Wilson, urging a no vote on this document, stating that all true friends of the treaty would stand against this compromise proposal. This letter angered McCumber, who thought it further proof that Wilson was behaving in a partisan manner.[49] McCumber was the last to speak on the subject before the vote took place, turning much of his anger on the Democrats for their behavior. McCumber told them that he could vote for the altered document, because, as he put it, the heart of the treaty remained. He then voted for the revised document. It got a majority but failed of a two-thirds vote.

After a series of parliamentary moves, Lodge allowed the original version--one that still read exactly the way it had when Wilson brought it home from Paris. It too failed of the necessary two-thirds vote because only loyalist Democrats voted for it--as did Porter J. McCumber. He was the only senator on November 19, 1919, to vote for both versions of the treaty.

Although the fight for the League of Nations was one of McCumber's two important moments on the political stage (the fight over the tariff that bears his name being the other), he disappeared from public view after November. He spent most of the time until the first of the year in Arizona with his wife and daughter, both of whom were ill.[50] Conferences involving Hitchcock and moderate leaders, some of whom were highly indignant about the failure of the treaty, took place with McNary and Lenroot.

McCumber was absent early in December when the Senate Foreign Relations Committee voted to send the infamous "smelling expedition" to the White House to determine if Woodrow Wilson, still recovering from his stroke, was able to function as president. Hitchcock, the only senator to see Wilson during the preceding months, tried to prevent it, but the committee voted 6 to 5 to send a delegation, headed by Albert Fall of New Mexico. Had McCumber been present, he might well have voted against such a matter. It should be remembered that on procedural questions pertaining to the League and related matters, he followed an independent course.[51]

McCumber was away during much of the new year as well. Therefore, he had no role in the attempts to develop a bipartisan committee to explore new approaches. He would not have been on the committee, because Lodge, who picked the Republican members, kept the moderates, save for Kellogg and Lenroot away from it.[52] He did not vote on the treaty on March 20, when the Senate made another attempt, once again falling short, although by now a number of Democratic defections had swelled the ranks of those willing to accept the document with the Lodge reservations attached. However, loyal Democrats and Irreconcilables still provided a sufficient margin to deny the necessary two-thirds vote. During the period between the November vote and the final vote in March, McCumber was rarely in the capital.[53] As Margulies wrote, the North Dakotan was now isolated from his colleagues on the subject, and his presence would hardly have mattered.[54]

McCumber concluded that the treaty was dead. In a statement he made in late December, he said that the time had come to explore new options.[55] He was not too specific, however, being distracted largely by the illnesses in his family which now took up much of his time. He returned to the Senate shortly after the vote, in time to participate in the debate over a resolution to terminate the war between the United States and the Central Powers. Knox introduced a motion to counter an earlier House proposal, but it did little more than simply bring the war to a close while reserving future actions for the United States. Presented in the Foreign Relations Committee, the motion passed on a strict partisan vote, with the Democrats continuing to fight the Versailles Treaty fight all over again. While McCumber voted to report the Knox proposal out, he did not follow a strict party line on the floor.

McCumber saw the whole issue as an exercise in futility. There would be no way that the Congress could override a presidential veto that would be sure to follow passage. He would prefer a resolution restoring commercial relations between the two countries and let other matters wait until later. He was not around for the vote, in which only Nelson broke party ranks to vote with the Democrats. The House then approved the Senate version, the president vetoed the measure, and the House, which had the first opportunity at override failed to do so.[56]

Of greater interest to McCumber was an effort to insert a plank in the Republican platform which would commit the United States to an international organization. By now, the party was sufficiently split on the League (as well as on a Republican candidate) that this proposal would have been an even more herculean task than getting an amended document past Woodrow Wilson. Nonetheless, with such senators as Kellogg and Lenroot, he lent himself to this effort. The end result was not successful, and presidential nominee Warren Harding, who had been a "strong reservationist," came out for an "association of nations" as a substitute for the League.[57]

McCumber's role in the treaty fight as noted earlier, has attracted a great deal of praise. He scored both sides of the dispute for their partisanship, stubbornness, and unwillingness to give the other side any credit for intellectual honesty. His one error was his willingness to line up with the Lodge "strong reservationists" in the fall of 1919 rather than adhere to a more independent course. Had he chosen to keep the "mild reservationists" united on this independent course, a difficult task at best, he might have provided the basis for a middle of the road approach that could have obliged Wilson and Lodge to accommodate, leaving only the Irreconcilables isolated. The same criticism could apply to Hitchcock, another midwestern internationalist who, like McCumber, allowed partisanship to creep into his strategy when a departure from this standard would have been in order. It would not be fair to say that McCumber's failure to do so was entirely without justification, and it would be similarly unfair to say that, by agreeing to sponsor a Lodge-endorsed version of Article X he caused the treaty to fail. He could not have altered history, even had he stuck to the "high road" that writers frequently mention in their analysis of McCumber's role in the dispute over the treaty.

NOTES

1. Elwyn Robinson, *History of North Dakota* (Lincoln: University of Nebraska Press, 1966), pp. 363-364; Paul Morrison, "The Position of Senators from North Dakota on Isolation, 1889-1920," Ph.D. thesis, University of Colorado, 1954, p. 272.

2. Eric Goldman, *Rendezvous With Destiny* (New York: Alfred A. Knopf, 1953), p. 186; John Milton Cooper, *The Vanity of Power: American Isolationism and World War I* (Westport, Conn.: Greenwood Press, 1969), pp. 179 and 220-224.

3. Thomas Bailey, *Woodrow Wilson and the Lost Peace* (New York: Macmillan Co., 1945), p. 206.

4. Ralph Stone, *The Irreconcilables* (Lexington: University of Kentucky Press, 1970), pp. 97-98.

5. Thomas Bailey, *Woodrow Wilson and the Great Betrayal* (New York: Macmillan Co., 1944), pp. 72-73.

6. Stone, pp. 183-187.

7. Herbert Margulies, *The Mild Reservationists and the League of Nations Controversy in the Senate* (Columbia: University of Missouri Press, 1989), p. xii. See also pp. 274 et seq.

8. Lloyd Ambrosius, *Woodrow Wilson and the American Diplomatic Tradition* (Middlesex: Cambridge Press, 1987), pp. 153-154.

9. Morrison, p. 253.

10. John Garraty, *Henry Cabot Lodge, A Biography* (New York: Alfred A. Knopf, 1953), p. 348.

11. *New York Times*, March 4, 1919, p. 2. See also Denno Fleming, *The United States and the League of Nations, 1918-1920* (New York: Russell and Russell, 1932), pp. 84 et seq. and Alan Cranston, *The Killing of the Peace* (New York: Viking Press, 1945), pp. 52-53.

12. *New York Times*, February 27, 1919, p. 2.

13. Ibid., March 4, 1919, p. 3. Fleming, pp. 148 et seq.

14. Quoted in Fleming, p. 152.

15. Ibid., pp. 153-155.

16. Belle and Fola LaFollette, *Robert M. LaFollette, June 14, 1855-June 18, 1925*, vol 2 (New York: Macmillan Co., 1953), p. 948.

17. Ibid., pp. 909-930. The Vice President Thomas Marshall is not to be confused with the Thomas Marshall of North Dakota politics.

18. Ibid., pp. 929-930.

19. Stone, pp. 97-99.

20. Morrison, pp. 282-283.

21. *New York Times*, June 10, 1919, pp. 1-2. See also Cranston, pp. 117-118.

22. Ibid., July 11, 1919, p. 1, July 12, 1919, p. 1, and July 14, 1919, p. 1.

23. Bailey, *The Great Betrayal*, pp. 74-77 and p. 376.

24. Margulies, p. 51.

25. See the letter from Taft to Hitchcock dated July 21, 1919, found in the Hitchcock papers (Library of Congress).

26. Marion McKenna, *Borah* (Ann Arbor: University of Michigan Press, 1961), p. 157.

27. *New York Times*, August 14, 1919, p. 4.

28. Ibid.

29. Herbert Margulies, *Senator Lenroot of Wisconsin: A Political Biography* (Columbia: University of Missouri Press, 1977), pp. 273 et seq.

30. Nicholas Murray Butler, *Across the Busy Years*, vol. 1 (New York: Charles Scribner and Sons, 1939), p. 197.

31. *New York Times*, August 25, 1919, p. 2. Fleming, pp. 326 et seq.; Henry Ashurst, *A Many Colored Toga: The Diary of Henry Fountain Ashurst* (Tucson: University of Arizona Press, 1962), pp. 102-103, and Cranston, pp. 165-166.

32. New York Times, August 27, 1919, p. 10. See also Fleming, pp. 326-327 and Cranston, p. 165.

33. Margulies, *League of Nations*, p. 125.

34. Morrison, p. 264.

35. Henry Cabot Lodge, *The United States Senate and the League of Nations* (New York: Charles Scribner and Sons, 1925), pp. 331-333.

36. Ibid., p. 325.

37. Ibid., pp. 319-320.

38. Ibid., pp. 310-311.

39. Ambrosius, p. 175.

40. Bailey, *The Great Betrayal*, pp. 393-394 shows the difference between Wilson's original and Hitchcock's changes.

41. Ibid., p. 152. See also Cranston, p. 177 and Fleming, pp. 363-365.

42. Ashurst, pp. 104-105.

43. Garraty, p. 376 and Lodge, pp. 183-185.

44. Stone, pp. 141-142.

45. Margulies, *League of Nations*, pp. 145-147.

46. Stone, pp. 141-142.

47. Cranston, p. 210.

48. *New York Times*, November 18, 1919, pp. 1-2 and Morrison, pp. 314-315.

49. See the *New York Times*, November 20, 1919, p. 1 for Wilson's letter. See also Morrison, pp. 317-319.

50. Margulies, *League of Nations*, p. 191.

51. *New York Times*, December 6, 1919, pp. 1-2.

52. For the bipartisan committee, see H.M. Darling, "Who Kept the United States Out of the League of Nations," *Canadian Historical Association* 10 (1929).

53. Margulies, *League of Nations*, p. 224.

54. Ibid.

55. Fleming, p. 471.

56. Ambrosius, pp. 254-257.

57. Margulies, *Lenroot*, p. 321.

5

The Fordney-McCumber Tariff

The year 1920 witnessed the zenith of the Republican party, especially its conservative faction. In control of both houses of Congress and the presidency, Republicans could credit their good fortune to the general disillusionment that occurred at the end of World War I. The war produced both a strong sense of nationalism and a return to the isolationism that favored them. The Democratic party was blamed for the war and for every economic evil, whether accurate or not. They also suffered because of their association with labor and because of the role they allowed labor leaders to play during the war as major strikes hit the country and caused nightmares about a possible "Bolshevik uprising." For the most part, however, it was the war, which by now most Americans believed had not been fought for "peace without victory" and "to make the world safe for democracy," but for the benefit of munitions makers and greedy national leaders who sought additional colonies and territories. Forgotten was the advocacy of most Republican leaders for a quick entry into the war and for a harsh and punitive peace.

Porter McCumber was one of the Republican leaders who profited from the party's success. He was now the second ranking Republican on the powerful Senate Finance Committee. He also chaired the somewhat less powerful, though still influential, Pensions Committee that would allow him access to a new and powerful force in American politics, World War I veterans. For a time, until Lodge moved to consolidate his own political power, he chaired the party's steering committee and he served on the party committee on committees. However, McCumber's successes and power lay solely at the national level, for back in North

Dakota matters were not going well for him.   The victory of the
candidates endorsed by the Non-Partisan League in 1916 had ushered in
a period in the state of that faction's domination of politics with their
call for a new social and economic order.   The most powerful figure in
the state was now Arthur Townley, not Alexander McKenzie.
McKenzie, even in his periods of greatest strength, never had Townley's
ability to summon all the legislators who were loyal to him to his hotel
in the state capital and impose a kind of caucus rule on them.

Therefore, McCumber, a conservative whose views lay at the other
end of the political spectrum from Townley and his followers, was a man
totally out of step with the dominant political force in his state.   He may
have owed his 1916 reelection partially to Townley's refusal to support
Burke, but this in no way suggested that those who looked to the Non-
Partisan League for leadership view him favorably.

The new leader included Lynn Frazier, who was elected governor
in 1916 and, in many ways, was typical of the new breed of North
Dakota politicians.   Born in Minnesota, he had turned to farming after
a brief career in law and joined with the Non-Partisan League in 1915.
Because of his reputation, he moved to the forefront of the movement
and was the candidate for governor in 1916, 1918, and 1920.   He would
win all three times, only to be impeached during his last term by a more
conservative legislature, a consideration that would work to his advantage
in 1922 when he would challenge McCumber for the Republican Senate
nomination.   Now he was a rural martyr to thousands of North Dakotans
who saw sinister conspiracies at work in the forces opposing the Non-
Partisan League.

William Lemke was another key figure.   More of an organizer
during this phase of his career, he was a product of Georgetown and
Yale, who still maintained a powerful hold over the farmers who flocked
to the movement.   A strong opponent of entry into World War I by the
United States, he would eventually go to the House of Representatives
and run in 1936 for the presidency as the candidate of the last remnants
of agrarian radicalism.

William Langer would enjoy an even longer and more colorful
career.   He had graduated from the university at fifteen and had gone on
to study law at Columbia University.   In 1914 he had become state's
attorney for Morton County where he quickly established the sort of
reputation that endeared him to progressives.   Ultimately, he would split
with the movement, but he would go on to become governor (during
which time he was indicted, convicted, and eventually cleared of
kickback charges) and United States senator.   A thoroughgoing
isolationist, he would be one of three senators (the dying Hiram Johnson
was another) to vote against U.S. involvement in the United Nations.

Langer would run for the governorship against Frazier in 1920 and lose, although the Non-Partisan League-endorsed candidates would not fare as well as would the heads of their ticket. The League itself would eventually fade out of existence, but the principles of agrarian radicalism that it represented would remain a significant part of the North Dakota political picture. Townley himself would resign the presidency of the organization in 1922, probably to save himself from being thrown out of the leadership of a group he had created. For a new breed of North Dakota agrarian radicals, he had become too much of a conservative and an accommodator.

Before the Non-Partisan League faded, it claimed other victims. One of these victims was Asle Gronna who was defeated for renomination by Dr. Edwin Ladd, former president of Agricultural College in 1920. That Gronna would lose to a candidate representing a more vigorous strain of agrarian radicalism is highly ironic. The old progressive would have nothing to do with the Non-Partisan League and went so far as to denounce it--even more so than did McCumber who seems to have been reluctant to come out strongly on the subject. The record of North Dakota's junior senator was not sufficient to save him from defeat.

The Non-Partisan League adopted a strong platform in the 1920s stressing ownership of terminal elevators, state inspection of grain dockage facilities, and exemption of farm improvements from taxation--a return to the platform of the early populists. They had become more internationalist in foreign affairs and had supported Wilson's efforts in the postwar period. In a previous chapter it was noted that public opinion in North Dakota tended to support McCumber's efforts on behalf of American entry into the League of Nations.[1]

McCumber angered them when he voted to return the railroads to their former owners (the Esch-Cummins Bill). Many progressive forces, happy that the roads had been taken over during the war, wanted them retained under government control, but the state's senior senator, fearful of socialism in any form, was a strong advocate of return. It was consistent with his political philosophy but clearly inconsistent with the sentiments of those North Dakotans who advocated government ownership of utilities and public carriers. Another test of faith occurred when LaFollette tried to block the nomination of John Esch, Republican of Wisconsin and co-author of the act, to the Interstate Commerce Commission. McCumber voted for the nominee.[2] None of this went over well with the Non-Partisan League or other reform elements of the state.

McCumber also stuck with the conservative faction in the Senate when he voted for seating Truman Newberry as senator from Michigan. Newberry, a Republican, whose expenditure of money in the campaign seemed excessive by the standards of the time, found his seat contested by Democrats as well as a number of Republican progressives including Borah, Norris, LaFollette, and Kenyon. To progressives, the fight might be over one specific seat, but there was the larger issue of the question of money politics. Eventually, some three years after the election, Newberry resigned, having won the right to sit but not the moral authority.[3]

McCumber did support the progressive position on woman suffrage, voting for the Nineteenth Amendment in 1919. It represented a sharp departure from an earlier stance; in 1914 he announced his opposition on constitutional grounds, contending that he did not believe that the national government should dictate to the states what voting qualifications should be. Some noted at the time that his view on federal intervention changed when other matters were before the Senate, for he continued to call for federal inspection and grading of grains produced within the states. North Dakota had limited suffrage for women as far back as 1880, although full suffrage was to be denied in a referendum.[4] Otherwise, his views on domestic issues remained consistent with those of the Republican leadership. His was one of the strongest voices on behalf of fiscal conservatism; in 1920 he warned his colleagues in the upper chamber that the federal deficit was out of control and would soon reach $2 billion. Government appropriations, he admonished them, should be cut to the bone and, with a gesture in the direction of his constituents, he added that the import of grain would have to be prohibited in order to allow the farmers to survive.

McCumber continued his general policy of internationalism during the three years in the 1920s when he served in the Senate. He argued against the efforts of Borah and others to reintroduce the Panama Tolls question, terming their efforts to abandon the principle of treating all countries alike to be a breach of faith. He likened their attitude to Germany's cavalier disregard of treaties, typified by its sweep through Belgium in 1914 in order to outflank the French.[5]

McCumber continued to argue on behalf of the World Court, international arbitration, and disarmament. Initially, he was somewhat leery about the Washington Naval Conference of 1921 and perhaps frustrated in some measure by the failure of his own efforts to bring about peace through negotiations. Once the conference began, he became an enthusiastic supporter of Secretary of State Charles Evans Hughes's plan for a naval holiday, commenting that this was the most encouraging sign in the conference to date.[6] He voted for the Four Power Pact in March, the most controversial proposal to come out of the meeting.[7] Interestingly, this vote was a reprise of the debate over the Versailles Treaty. This time, however, it was the Republicans who were defending the president's actions and the Democrats who were asking for more details before they would approve ratification. This time, however, the president, Harding, had taken the step of appointing senators, including Underwood and Lodge, to the delegation.

During the course of the debate, McCumber raised the question as to why the Republicans had "scrapped" the idea of an association of nations which they had raised during the fight over the Versailles Treaty. No senator on the majority side of the aisle had an answer for him. Despite this foray into the past, McCumber remained loyal to the purpose and principles of the conference. Its most important development, he commented at one point, was that the United States was playing the role of "World Conscience."[8]

THE EMERGENCY TARIFF ACT, 1921

When World War I began in 1914, the United States had already passed the Tariff Act, which marked the return to the moderate tariffs of the pre-Civil War period, though protectionists as usual predicted dire consequences for the economy, public sentiment generally favored the bill. The Democrats, as expected in an off-year election, lost some seats in the House of Representatives but maintained their absolute dominance in the Senate. To all appearances in 1914, the country desired a moderate tariff bill.[9]

The Tariff Act of 1913 remained in effect for nine years. When we look at the dates of the tariff acts of the preceding forty years, 1883, 1890, 1894, 1897, and 1909, we find that only the Dingley Bill of 1897 had a longer life. Some might attribute this to the demise of protectionist sentiment; however, such was not the case. Protectionism never died but remained dormant to the urgency of conducting the war. The protectionists allowed the war to accomplish their task for them by eliminating, to a great extent, the importation of foreign goods. At the same time, American exporters had less difficulty finding neutral markets for their goods. But the war would not last forever, and the cry of protectionism would be raised again. [10]

With the election of Harding in 1920, the protectionists who had opposed the Underwood-Simmons downward revision in 1913, once again, found themselves sitting in a position of power. Their arguments for upward tariff revision would be based on both economics and nationalism. The economics were quite simple. The prosperity that occurred during the war was due to few foreign imports and to the abundance of American exports as a result of the war and not the tariff. Now that the war was over and the expectation of imports a reality, the United States should protect its prosperity by keeping out foreign goods.

The protectionists could now use this intense nationalistic feeling to rationalize the upper revision of the tariff.[11]

Demand for revision of the Underwood-Simmons Tariff came shortly after the 1920 election. In early January, 1921, Joseph W. Fordney of Michigan, chairman of the House Ways and Means Committee, guided an emergency tariff bill through the House of Representatives. The Democrats opposed the bill claiming that it would not raise enough revenue to justify it and that it would close most world markets to American goods. The Republicans, on the other hand, cared little about revenue raising and justified their support for the bill on the grounds that it would help end the recession that was plaguing the country. In early February Fordney claimed that the current recession could be explained in terms of the insufficient duty rates of the Underwood-Simmons Tariff. These rates had to rise in order to deal with the high cost of production in this country. According to him, the disparity between production costs in the United States and abroad was greater than before the war.[12]

On January 17, 1921, Boies Penrose, chairman of the Senate Finance Committee, reported the bill to the Senate. Penrose was not well and depended a great deal on McCumber to guide the bill in the full chamber. From the outset, McCumber made it known that the House version of the bill was not protective enough, especially in the area of wheat. Wheat had been taxed at 25 cents a bushel in the Payne Bill in 1909 and then put on the free list in the Underwood Bill in 1913. The House imposed a 35 cents a bushel tariff in 1921, but McCumber, in the Senate version, was able to raise it to 50 cents a bushel. He was concerned about the large amounts of wheat imported from Canada.[13]

On February 24 the conference committee agreed on a single version of the tariff bill, which was passed by the House on February 26 by a vote of 205 to 127 and two days later by the Senate by a vote of 49 to 36. Although eleven Democrats in the Senate voted with the Republicans, it would not be enough to override an almost certain veto by outgoing President Wilson. The president, an opponent of the Payne-Aldrich Bill of 1909, claimed that the new tariff was its reincarnation, and even the Republicans did not deny that fact. The majority party made no secret that the emergency tariff should resemble the Payne bill as much as possible. When we compare the two bills in terms of some of the major agricultural items, we find little difference. For instance, wheat was 10 cents more a bushel in the new bill, and the tariffs on corn, butter, potatoes, milk and cream did not change at all. However, the big surprise was that the agricultural sector, which generally opposed protective tariffs, fearing retaliation and higher nonfarm domestic prices, was now calling for protection too. The decline of the prices of wheat, corn, meats, and cotton in 1920 to one-third of their war-time values, due to overproduction, foreign imports, and the loss of the European market, was enough of an impetus for agriculture to support the Emergency Tariff Act. The farm sector, in return for higher duties on its products, had agreed to support a tariff on dyestuffs, tungsten, magnesite, chemical and optical glassware, and surgical instruments. Most of these products were not protected in 1909 since the United States did not have a chemical industry and depended on foreign importation. However, during the First World War, its chemical industry grew tremendously, primarily as a result of the takeover of German chemical factories operating on its shores. Therefore, in the postwar period, these new chemical industries did not want any competition.[14]

Another major change from the Payne-Aldrich Bill was the new proposal's antidumping provision. This provision would prevent foreign companies from selling their products in the United States below cost. Even though this measure never passed, the principle is embodied in the Anti-Dumping Act of 1921. This act empowered the United States International Trade Commission, after protest by domestic producers, to slap antidumping duties on foreign goods.[15]

On March 3, only days before leaving office, Wilson vetoed the Emergency Tariff Bill. In his final message to Congress, he stated that it was no time to erect high tariff barriers that would interfere with American business at home and abroad. The president was clearly concerned about foreign retaliation when he declared that it was time to widen world markets and not to contract them. The president, like his fellow Democrats, attacked the imposition of high duties on agricultural goods, contending that they would raise the cost of living in the United States. The cost of sugar would rise from $7.35 per hundred pounds to $9.00 per hundred pounds. An increase in the tariff on apples of 300 percent was perceived as foolish since the country only imported on the average about $50,000 worth while exporting $10 million.[16]

The Republicans expected Wilson's veto of the Emergency Tariff Bill. Although they failed to override it in the House by twenty two votes, they had every intention of reintroducing the bill as soon as the more friendly Warren Harding assumed the presidency. In less than three weeks after Wilson's veto, another Emergency Tariff Bill was introduced in both houses of Congress. However, by late April and early May 1921, it seemed that the bill might be in trouble in the Senate because the House had failed to add the antidumping provision and an embargo on dyestuffs. The major supporters of the antidumping provision were from the eastern manufacturing section of the country, while there was little support for it in the West. The dyestuff embargo was a particular concern of the chemical industry.[17]

On May 4, 1921, Simmons spoke against the bill as a whole but especially the antidumping provision. He tried to show that the antidumping provision could lead to retaliation by foreign countries. He urged his fellow senators to vote against the entire bill. McCumber responded to Simmons by praising the bill as a whole, and, though supporting the antidumping provision, he played down its importance. McCumber stated, "I have looked into the anti-dumping section from all angles. I admit candidly that it will do little good and I am certain it will do little harm."[18]

On May 11 just prior to the Senate vote, Hitchcock made a speech condemning the dyestuff embargo provision that Penrose added to the Senate bill on April 30. The Nebraskan referred to the dyestuff industry as a powerful trust with large business interests in both the United States and Europe. Despite vehement opposition, the Senate passed the Emergency Tariff Bill with the dyestuff embargo and the antidumping provision by a vote of 63 to 28. Three days later, the House voted on the same bill, minus the antidumping provision and the dyestuff embargo, and passed it by a vote of 238 to 98. On May 18, a conference committee reached a compromise on the bill, keeping the antidumping provision and reducing the dyestuff embargo provision from a period of six months, the length of the Emergency Tariff, to three months. On May 27 Harding signed essentially the same tariff bill that Wilson had vetoed in March. The bill was supposed to last only six months, at which time it would be replaced by a permanent tariff bill. However, it lasted much longer, for it was not until September, 1922, or sixteen months later, that the Fordney-McCumber Bill was ready for Harding's signature.[19]

On May 29, only two days after Harding signed the Emergency Tariff law, Frank Taussig, former chairman of the Tariff Commission and an expert on tariff and trade, commented on the effects of a high protective tariff on world trade. Taussig pointed out that since World War I the United States had been a creditor nation accumulating most of the gold supply in the world. If the United States expected foreign nations to pay their debts and financial obligations, he said, the country must increase its imports relative to its exports. By erecting a tariff barrier and keeping foreign goods from entering the country, the United States was contributing to the eventual economic ruin of Europe. Taussig pointed out that foreign countries viewed the country's tariff policy as paradoxical. On the one hand, the United States professed support for an open door policy and then it shut its door in everybody's face.[20]

THE FORDNEY TARIFF BILL

Fordney began preparing a new tariff bill in early June, 1921. At first the Republicans held open hearings on the necessity of a new tariff bill. The majority party members of the House Ways and Means Committee were not always in agreement on everything. For instance, there was difficulty over the lumber schedule. The Minnesota delegation to the House was at odds with Chairman Fordney over the 25 percent ad valorem duty on lumber. They wanted lumber placed on the free list and wrote Harding urging him to support their position. John McClury of the Master Carpenters Association also sent a letter to Chairman Fordney echoing the demands of the Minnesota delegations. Eventually, lumber was placed on the free list.[21]

By June 28 a bill consisting of about 300 pages representing six months' work by the House Ways and Means Committee was ready for House action. Debate was held to a minimum by a special "gag" rule that limited amendments from the floor to members of the House Ways and Means Committee and required a final vote by July 21. The House tariff bill as it stood would raise the average duty to nearly 56 percent and raise $700 million in revenue for the government.[22]

One of the most controversial parts of the House tariff bill was the provision for an American Valuation Plan supported by Fordney to determine the ad valorem rates. Simply put, an invoice of imports would have to contain a statement of the exporter abroad of the cost price of the imported article, together with a statement of the actual money values in the country of origin. These money values would then be compared at the Customs House in the United States with the values in American dollars and the value of the goods would be determined on that basis. The objective behind this plan was to apply ad valorem rates to American valuation of the products, which was generally higher than foreign valuation, which had been the custom in the past.[23]

The rates of Fordney Bill in the House were noticeably higher than those of the Payne-Aldrich Bill of 1909 and much higher than those of the Underwood-Simmons Bill of 1913. For example, in the Underwood-Simmons Bill wool was placed on the free list, while in the Payne-Aldrich Bill it was 44 cents a pound. The Fordney version called for a 60 percent ad valorem rate. Hides were also placed on the free list in the Underwood Bill and remained so until the bill reached the House floor in July, 1921 when Republicans split over the issue. Many Republicans from the cattle raising states wanted a 15 percent ad valorem duty on hides, and for the next week, a battle raged in the House over the issue.[24]

Although lumber stayed on the free list in the Fordney Bill, paper board, pulp board, sugar candies, paints, and coal tar products were all increased in the new bill. For example, sugar candies were 25 percent ad valorem in the Underwood version and 30 percent in the Fordney Bill. Coal tar products, including dyes, went up from 5 percent ad valorem to 30 percent ad valorem, and paper board and pulp increased from 5 to 10 percent. Other articles that were on the free list in the Underwood Bill such as arsenic, carbolic and fluoric acids, bauxite, beeswax, gloves, lard compounds, leather cut for shoes, limestone rock, asphalt, nails, orange and lemon peel, paper stock, printing paper, wafers, wheat, and wheat floor were now all dutiable items. As a result of pressure exerted by the growing chemical industry in the United States, the embargo on dye products, part of the Emergency Tariff Bill, was continued in the Fordney Bill.[25]

The Democrats wasted little time attacking the Fordney Bill when it reached the House for consideration. Led by Claude Kitchin, they called the tariff bill a plan to plunder the American people; they claimed that it would cost every man, woman, and child $20 a year. Kitchin called the tariff bill a conspiracy to benefit favorite industries that supported the Republican party; it was framed to finance the party by repaying contributors for past campaigns. The Democrats claimed that the rates in the Fordney Bill were the highest ever if the American valuation system were included. John Nance Garner of Texas, the Democratic leader in the House, seized a straw hat and challenged any Republican to state the duty on it. He maintained that the duty on the straw hat was 50 percent ad valorem in the Payne-Aldrich Bill, but in the Fordney Bill it was $10 a dozen, plus an ad valorem duty of 20 percent, which made the import tax 61 percent. Republicans reminded Garner that he had voted for the Emergency Tariff Bill in 1921, but "Cactus Jack" was quick to admit that he had made a mistake. The Texas Democrat went on to condemn the American valuation system and the tariff, predicting that it would raise the cost of living in the United States considerably.[26]

Fordney defended the bill by declaring that the Underwood Bill had been a failure and that tariff revision was long overdue. He claimed that the new bill would protect the American farmer and provide more jobs for American labor. He also contended that the new tariff bill would help the servicemen returning from the war find employment, and he predicted disaster for the economy if it failed to pass. He emphasized that the protection of the American market against the revival of European industry should become the nation's first priority, and he gave examples of how goods found their way to the United States from Germany and Japan for less than the American cost of production.[27]

Fordney achieved the passage of the tariff bill on July 21 by a vote of 289 to 127. Only seven Republicans voted against the measure, including James Sinclair from North Dakota. On the other hand, seven

Democrats voted in favor of the bill. In its final form, the Fordney Bill kept hides, lumber, oil, cotton, and asphalt on the free list, ended the embargo on dyestuff and declared for the American valuation system. [28]

During the House debate on the Fordney Bill, the foreign governments of Argentina and Spain protested vehemently against what they believed would be in the new tariff. It was a harbinger of things to come. The Argentinean government announced that it was in the process of passing retaliatory legislation, while the Spanish government sent the American Chamber of Commerce in Spain a copy of its new tariff bill that would considerably reduce American exports to Spain. The Spanish government was preparing for a world tariff war that it blamed on the United States. [29]

The Fordney Bill, similar to the Emergency Tariff Bill, which generally raised rates upward on agricultural and manufactured goods, was delayed in the Senate for more than a year. Hearings by the Senate Finance Committee began on July 22, only one day after the House disposed of the bill. Penrose remained uncertain whether the Committee should tackle the tax revision bill or the tariff bill first. He stated that, prior to any discussion of the Fordney rates, the committee should debate the American Evaluation Plan first. President Harding favored tax revision as a priority over tariff revision and had doubts about implementing the American Evaluation Plan. [30]

From July 23 until August 27, when the tariff bill was put aside for tax revision, the Senate Finance Committee focused on two major issues: the American Evaluation Plan and the restoration of the dye embargo. Hearings on both issues took up most of the time. McCumber compared the American Evaluation Plan to wartime cost-plus contracts. He opposed the plan on the grounds that the disadvantages outweighed the advantages. On the other hand, Secretary of Commerce Herbert Hoover lauded both the American Valuation Plan and the restoration of the dye embargo. Hoover was determined to protect American industry against foreign dumping. [31]

One of the more important issues that arose during the Senate debate was raised by the chemical and dye industry which favored restoration of the dye embargo. During the Senate Finance Committee hearings in August, 1921, a number of witnesses representing the dye industry warned that should the embargo be lifted, their firms would be destroyed by German competition. They wanted to continue the Emergency Tariff embargo on all dye imports for at least another five years. Two days after the hearings on the dye embargo, Harding agreed to extend it for only another three months. [32]

On August 27, Boies Penrose announced that the committee would delay the tariff bill and take up the tax bill. There appeared to be two major reasons for this decision. Harding favored quick action on the tax bill, and the Finance Committee needed more time to study the American valuation system.   The committee asked experts on the Tariff Commission to study economic conditions abroad that might warrant implementing the system.[33]

On August 30, 1921, another threat of the tariff war was raised when Cuban minister, de Cespedes sent a formal memorandum to Secretary of State Charles Evans Hughes warning the United States about the future of American investments in Cuba should the sugar and tobacco duties be increased.   The Cuban government was irritated about the increase in sugar duties in the Emergency Tariff Bill which had cost the country $32 million.   Four months later, in December, massive demonstrations took place in Cuba as 30,000 people marched in protest to higher sugar duties. At the time of the march, the Finance Committee was considering raising the already high duty in the Fordney Bill, which was 1.6 cents a pound, to between 2 and 2.5 cents per pound. Exports from the United States to Cuba in 1914 were exceeded only by those to the United Kingdom, Canada, and France.[34]

In the closing months of 1921 the views of economists and business on the Fordney Tariff were heard on both sides of the ocean. In early November, seventy one economists opposed the bill, claiming that it would harm the country's welfare if it became law. It would not only decrease the country's trade but it would also be costly to administer. Several days after the poll was published, the National Garment Retailers Association wrote Penrose asking him to block the American Valuation Plan because it felt it would prove disastrous to the retail dry goods business.   One week later, Akira Ishii, president of Japan's Mall Steamship Company and G. Takikawa, president of the Kobe Chamber of Commerce who was known internationally as Japan's "Match King," denounced both the American Valuation Plan and the high rates of the Fordney Bill. Takikawa was attending the Washington Naval Conference in Washington when he made his comments: "A tariff war may breed an armed war. The Fordney bill increases certain customs duties and may create bad feelings in other countries. The United States will save $700 million under Hughes' proposal (for naval disarmament). Why could it not cut down on the Fordney schedules?"[35]   Takikawa pointed out that he never asked the Japanese government for tariffs to protect the many different types of manufactures in which he was interested.[36]

A special committee representing the United States Chamber of Commerce opposed the American Valuation Plan until world conditions improved. A spokesman for the committee stated that "tariff legislation should be framed and administered with a view to meeting discrimination direct or indirect by other countries against American trade."[37] Supporters of the American Valuation Plan were no less vocal. The National Association of Manufacturers stated unequivocally that the

American Valuation Plan was the salvation of American business and should be enacted at once. Fordney, concerned about the criticism of his plan, blamed the importers for trying to defeat the House legislation by deception. He claimed that "opposition to the tariff bill does not come from the American producer or the man who sells chiefly American made products, but from the man who produces abroad and the man whose chief interest is in bringing the product of cheap foreign labor to the American market."[38]

On January 1, 1922, Boies Penrose died. A large, high-living product of a well-to-do family, Penrose had practiced politics as though a product of the wards and became the "boss" of his native state. A brilliant and conservative man, he even managed to maintain decent political and personal relations with those insurgents who despised his politics and who had tried to upset the seniority system in 1919 to keep him from his just reward, the chairmanship of the Senate Finance Committee.[39]

While Penrose may be better known to the study of American politics as the quintessential "boss," he was also part of the close relationship between the Republican leadership and the eastern financial interests. It was largely through his instigation that Andrew Mellon became secretary of the Treasury in the Harding cabinet.[40] Penrose held the position to which the financial leaders believed that access was essential, one that had always been held by an easterner such as Nelson Aldrich of Rhode Island. The relationship to an earlier chairman was best epitomized by a remark Nelson Aldrich made in the aftermath of the 1917 money crisis: "We may not always have Pierpont Morgan with us to meet a banking crisis." [41]

Now there was a problem. No longer was an easterner with impeccable ties to the establishment in charge of a Republican dominated committee. Rather, the Chairman was from North Dakota--a somewhat unknown figure as far as many eastern bankers were concerned. Their concern was heightened by the growth of what historians have come to call the "farm bloc," a bipartisan group of senators and representatives who became almost a third party within the Congress and seemed to be outside the control of the leadership. Many of them had been elected with the aid of the Non-Partisan League, which had branched out from North Dakota and had managed to support winning candidates in other midwestern states as well. Some bankers were concerned because the League had given tacit consent to McCumber's reelection in 1916.[42]

There should have been no concern about the North Dakotan in business circles, nor did there appear to be any among his colleagues. Any early apostasy evident in his support of the Pure Food and Drug Act and a few other measures was more than compensated for by his regular stands on the tariff and his fiscal conservatism. McCumber moved immediately to dispel any worries about his regularity. On January 8, following the truce that had been called during the eulogies and funeral for Penrose, McCumber announced that he would not do anything to hold up consideration of the tariff bill. The previous Friday had marked the first anniversary of the hearings of the bill in the House Ways and Means Committee, and the Emergency Tariff Bill had been extended twice. Shortly before his death, Penrose had predicted that the new tariff bill was sure to clear the committee by June and be ready for the conference committee shortly thereafter. Nonetheless, McCumber found it necessary to "leak" the fact that he was solidly in favor of the measure and would push it.[43] The following day, the Republican Committee on Committees went through the formal process of recommending to the full party (and to the Senate) that McCumber succeed to the chairmanship of the Finance Committee.[44]

On January 19, McCumber released an article he had written shortly after he became chairman. It was designed to allay any fears on Wall Street that his state identification meant anything as far as their interests were concerned. He dismissed the idea of sectionalism as a factor in his makeup, and he argued that a westerner could be as good a protectionist as could someone with an Ivy League degree and Wall Street connections. If there had been any virtue in the past in pushing for lower tariff barriers, it was academic now. Keeping the present tariff in place would be ruinous to the economy, particularly to industry. Protectionism, he said, was to be maintained not as a sectional, but as a national policy. The East, he said, had not and would not suffer as a result of the growing western leadership in the Congress for all that the westerners wanted was their share of the opportunity. Under his leadership, McCumber told them, the Republican party would remain the party of protectionism. Noting the rise in production costs, he stated that anything else would be disastrous.[45]

McCumber stated that, ironically, in the West he was viewed as too conservative, whereas in the East it was thought that geography might make him a radical. He closed his remarks by alluding favorably to the soldier's bonus bill, which was presently before the Finance Committee and which he had been championing for some time. During his chairmanship of the Pensions Committee, a post he was now obliged to surrender, he had argued strenuously for this piece of legislation. This part of his letter did not please the easterners, for most of them opposed the bonus bill.

The factor that most allayed the fears of eastern bankers and industrialists was not so much the letter but the assurances by senators from that area that McCumber was sound. They learned to work effectively with him during his tenure as Finance Committee chairman, even though during much of this period he was a lame duck-leader, having been defeated for renomination in late June, at a time when the debate over the tariff was at its height. When McCumber spoke about the perception in the West that he was too conservative, he might have been peering into the future and the primary campaign in North Dakota.[46]

THE BONUS BILL

McCumber's leadership in the fight for tariff reform was compromised to some extent by his work on the soldier's bonus. It is difficult to determine which item held a greater priority for him during the period from January to September of 1922. As second-ranking member of the Finance Committee and chairman of the Pensions Committee, he had developed powerful contacts with veterans groups and other strong supporters of the bonus. And he was not unaware of the political implications of support for any legislator who worked hard for veterans benefits. In North Dakota, veterans' groups were not without influence or voice.

What fiscal conservatives worried most about in the pension bill was the matter of financing. McCumber had a solution, however. He looked to the interest payments on the foreign debt as the key to the country's ability to finance a bonus for veterans. He had begun his efforts in 1921, before Harding and the Republicans took power, when Wilson was waiting out the final days of his presidency. He proposed the bonus but withdrew it quickly in the face of opposition from the administration and leaders of his party including President-elect Harding and Secretary of the Treasury-designate Andrew Mellon. It was not a setback, for he expected this opposition. He was laying the groundwork for 1922.[47]

When he proposed it that year, the matter of funding was still vague. Harding was leery, and Mellon announced that nothing would be approved unless Congress guaranteed its funding.[48] The measure was then put on hold through much of the spring of 1922 while the new Finance Committee chairman and the Senate dealt with the tariff. However, McCumber still found time to play hookey from his new duties in this regard and met with veterans groups on the question of timing and the form of the bonus proposal. He encountered criticism from Democrats for leaving them out of the discussions.[49]

The criticism McCumber would encounter in managing the tariff were echoed by those who found fault with his activities on behalf of the pension bill. Whatever McCumber's talents, he had turned out to be a mediocre manager, or at least a mediocre manager of two major proposals at one time. Republican senators were incensed when he hinted at one point that he might sidetrack the tariff bill so as to emphasize the need for the soldier's bonus. In a White House conference with McCumber, Lodge, and others, Harding made it clear that he opposed it in its present form. However, McCumber took an optimistic view of the meeting and told senators that the bonus bill would be on the floor in a week and that the first installment of the interest on the British loan would provide the first installment of the payment of the bonus.[50] In a letter to Fordney, Harding said that he would veto any bill that did not provide for a sales tax as a means of financing.[51] The North Dakota senator was adamantly opposed to a sales tax.[52]

In June Harding was still strongly opposed to any bonus bill that did not make adequate provisions for financing, and he was equally opposed to sidetracking the tariff bill. So was the Republican caucus, which insisted on pushing the tariff bill at the expense of the bonus proposal, a position that angered McCumber who said that he would not be bound by the decision.[53] However, the next day after conferring with several other majority senators, he reversed himself and announced that a compromise had been struck. He would put the bonus bill aside until the tariff had been resolved--in exchange for a commitment that the legislature would not adjourn until it had been passed.[54] He also told his colleagues on the floor that he was convinced that Harding would sign the bill.

The bonus did not pass the Senate until the fall of 1922--by a margin of 36 to 17--a seemingly veto-proof margin. McCumber was certain that the president would sign the bill.[55] The final product was a measure that gave each veteran a paid-up certificate that would compound from its original value three times after twenty years. That it was still controversial is reflected in the failure of forty three senators to show up for the vote.[56]

Harding vetoed the bill, expressing sympathy for the veterans but concerned that the financing would increase the public debt. It was an unusually (for him) courageous political act, given the tremendous lobbying effort mounted by the veterans. McCumber now had to pin his hopes on the override, and the House of Representatives did just this, leaving the matter to the Senate. However, when the upper chamber got around to voting on the measure, they rejected it. Forty four voted in favor, but twenty-eight were opposed, eight more than necessary to uphold the president's veto. McCumber complained that some senators favored the bonus but were afraid to cross the president of their party and thus had absented themselves from the final ballot.[57]

The day after the Senate upheld the president's veto, the chief executive signed the tariff bill into law. It would be difficult to state which of these actions had the greatest importance for McCumber.[58]

THE FORDNEY-McCUMBER TARIFF

On January 9, John H. Kirby of Houston, Texas, and president of the Southern Tariff Association, spoke before the Finance Committee. He attacked many of the southern politicians who were opposed to the high tariff and stated unequivocally that "we are not following our politicians on the issue any longer."[59] Kirby claimed that somebody had to take a stand against the cheap goods that foreign countries were exporting. Charles B. Claiborne, a banker from New Orleans and another member of the Southern Tariff Association, claimed that 90 percent of the southern bankers favored a high protective tariff, a fact that was not substantiated.[60]

On the following day, January 10, Harding spoke before the Southern Tariff Association and declared that a high protective tariff was necessary to protect all sections of the country as well as businessmen, workers, and farmers. In doing so, Harding was echoing McCumber who had previously called the tariff a national rather than a sectional issue. It was obvious from the statements made by Kirby the day before that the Republicans felt they had the opportunity to appear as the national party on the tariff issue and to score points against the Democrats in the next election.[61]

From January 10 until April 11, the Finance Committee spent their time rewriting the Fordney Bill. The major issue at hand was the American Valuation Plan in the House bill. At first it appeared that opposition to the plan was mounting in the committee, owing to the existence of pressure groups such as the Wholesale Dry Goods Association and the Consumers Committee of Women, a nonpolitical and noncommercial committee representing women voters of the country. Both organizations made known their opposition to the plan. The Consumers Committee of Women pointed out that, if the American Valuation Plan in the House version was adopted, it would lead to increased living costs at home, destroy export markets and foreign trade, and bring foreign retaliation.[62]

Fordney closely followed the proceedings of the Finance Committee, especially those pertaining to the American Valuation Plan. On February 18, he warned members of the Senate committee that if they failed to maintain the plan in the bill, the House would write a new bill and let the Senate try again until they did it his way. He said that he would refuse to compromise on this issue; he would never agree to any foreign valuation plan.[63]

On March 15, the Senate Finance Committee, largely because of the Farm Bloc's influence, voted to take hides off the free list and to impose a duty of 15 percent ad valorem. This was an extraordinary turn of events, for hides had been on the free list in the Payne-Aldrich Bill, the

Underwood-Simmons Bill, and the Fordney Bill. This matter would remain unresolved when the bill reached the Senate in April.[64]

On March 31, the committee agreed to continue the dye embargo for at least one year. The chemical industry had wanted a five- year embargo, arguing vigorously that one year was not long enough to protect them from German competition.[65] When the bill finally was reported out of committee on April 11, over 2,000 amendments had been added to the House version, the majority of them representing a greater protectionist position. It was estimated that the Senate Finance Committee version of the bill would raise $300 million to $350 million in revenue for the government, even with foreign valuation as the basis of the bill. The American Valuation Plan was defeated by the Finance Committee by a vote of 7 to 3 on April 8. However, in order to appease those like Fordney, who had made the statement that "it will be American Valuation or Congress will remain here until the snow flies,"[66] the Finance Committee gave President Harding authority to modify rates either upward or downward within prescribed limits. The president could change the basis for assessing ad valorem duties on selected items from the foreign value to the value of the domestic article in the American market when the foreign value was not a certain basis for assessment of duties on such items.[67]

On April 12, McCumber, pleased with the wheat rate being set at 30 cents a bushel in the Senate bill, raised 5 cents from the House version, defended the Senate tariff bill as "all-American." He spoke in glowing terms as to how the bill would revive the country's industry and trade by protecting its markets. He said, "We cannot import prosperity."[68] He also tried to defuse the American Valuation Plan issue, which was then raging between Republican Senator Reed Smoot of Utah and Fordney. Smoot, a leading opponent of American valuation, worked vigorously to impose the foreign valuation method in the Senate Finance Committee Bill. McCumber did not think the issue was worth arguing about since the president had been given the power to make changes when necessary.[69]

The bill was sent to the full Senate where the majority, including the farm bloc, supported the Senate Finance Committee's version of the bill. Once again, as in 1921, the farm bloc was led to believe that falling farm prices could be averted through protectionism. Senator Edwin Ladd of North Dakota spoke for them, threatening to resist any attempt to lower agricultural rates, including the duty on hides. He asserted that the farmers would not allow manufacturers to be the only beneficiaries of protectionism. If there was no duty on hides, he stated, then there should be none on shoes. When Furnifold Simmons of North Carolina pointed out that the high rates would reduce the farmers' exports, Ladd replied that the American farmer no longer depended on international markets for prosperity.[70]

This was a new position for farmers who had generally supported the Democratic low tariff argument, put forth by Wilson in 1919, that protective tariffs had nothing to do with the problems of the agricultural sector. Wilson had contended that the farmer needed a better system of marketing and credit and larger foreign markets for his surplus. However, by 1921 and again in 1922, the farmers were so desperate to stop falling agricultural prices that they took very seriously Ladd's statement, "the farmer today knows that protection spells the difference between prosperity and failure." [71]

By the beginning of May, McCumber was becoming extremely irritated by the slow progress of the tariff in the Senate. He predicted that, if the Senate persisted in debating every issue, the bill would not pass until the end of September, 1946. He also stated that night sessions might have to be ordered soon.[72] The major reason for this delay was the mounting opposition to the tariff in the press as well as in the Senate. The *New York Times* in a May 2 editorial lashed out against protectionism in general and against the duty on hides in particular. According to the paper, the United States Tariff Commission showed that every cent per pound of duty on hides translated into an additional price of 10 cents on a pair of shoes. The tariff on hides would raise consumer prices on leather goods and only strengthen and complete the packers' monopoly.[73]

On May 8, Walsh of Montana, Underwood, and Simmons called for a more flexible tariff. They asserted that the proposed tariff bill existed for the sole purpose of maintaining the profits of large corporations. Walsh also questioned the constitutionality of that section of the House bill which gave the president the power to raise and lower duties, contending that the Constitution gave this exclusive right to Congress.[74]

On May 10, the Senate held its first night session devoted exclusively to the tariff issue. Simmons professed not to understand the need for these sessions. He complained that the Republicans wanted to rush the bill through without serious discussion and debate. He shocked his fellow senators by calling the bill not so much a protective measure as one meant to exploit the American people for the benefit of specific business interests. Although Simmons failed to name these interests at the time, Hitchcock pointed his finger at the chemical and dye industry. He condemned the dye embargo and declared that it was directed solely against Germany for the purpose of destroying the import trade with that country.[75]

McCumber countered the attacks by his Democratic opponents, defending the night sessions as necessary because the Democrats were taking up too much time by asking for a detailed explanation of how the

Finance Committee arrived at every rate. He accused the Democrats of wanting to kill the bill by means of a filibuster. Simmons dismissed these charges as ridiculous, maintaining that the tariff bill did not have the broad support of the press and the public. To buttress his argument, he pointed to editorials in both the *Chicago Tribune* and *New York Journal of Commerce*. McCumber claimed that the majority of the press did not support free trade because they were controlled, through the medium of advertising, by the department stores and retailers who were against the tariff bill.[76]

By the middle of May, McCumber and his protectionist supporters recognized that the night sessions had failed to expedite the tariff legislation. Senate sessions began at 11:00 in the morning and did not end until 10:30 in the evening. These marathon sessions increased the amount of absenteeism and irritated the Finance Committee chairman. On May 17, McCumber stated in no uncertain terms that any senator who did not remain at his post should resign. Once again, he proclaimed that the bill would be kept before the Senate, no matter how long it took to pass.[77] On May 25, the Republican leadership, tired of the delay in the Senate, sought closure on the tariff issue. The Democrats, on the other hand, claimed closure was uncalled for since there was no filibuster in progress. Two days later, a vote on closure was defeated as many Republicans voted with the Democrats on this issue.[78]

On June 1, a near fistfight broke out between Senator McCumber and Democratic Senator Joseph Robinson of Arkansas over the subject of adjournment. Senator Robinson, during a night session, wanted to adjourn prior to a vote on the brick schedule while McCumber insisted that the vote be taken. The argument became so heated that both senators advanced toward the center aisle to meet each other when another senator stepped between them.[79]

On June 14, the protectionists in the Senate put on what Simmons called the "Big Republican Tariff Show." On that day, Republican Senator George McLean of Connecticut held up a cheap pocket knife made in Germany and claimed it would not cut cheese. Another senator was upset with foreign made-razors that he contended would not cut corn. And once again, McCumber proclaimed that newspapers opposed the tariff bill because they were under orders from their advertisers to do so. Both Hitchcock and The *New York Times* editorial page ridiculed McCumber for his statement on the advertisers. Hitchcock called McCumber's statement "idiotic" while The *New York Times* referred to it as "nonsense"[80]

One week after the "Big Republican Tariff Show," the Executive Committee of the National Retail Dry Goods Association criticized McCumber for his ignorance of the relationship between newspapers and advertisers. This organization, representing department stores and other retail outlets, stated emphatically that department stores were not profiteering and that newspapers were not subservient to them. They declared that McCumber, in assessing the profit made by retail establishments on foreign goods, tended to look only at the value of foreign goods and the price they sold for in the United States. McCumber assumed that if the foreign cost of an item was $1.00 and it retailed in the United States for $9.45, it would be argued that the spread or profit was $8.45. However, they said, McCumber did not take into consideration the cost of foreign buying, inland freight abroad, consular fees, freight and insurance, duty to the U.S. government, and custom-house charges.[81]

On June 27, Walsh lashed out at the farm bloc, accusing it of proposing changes that would add to the nation's inflation. He claimed that the higher rates on agricultural products (duties had been increased on many items from 20 to 350 percent) added to the cost of food. In the Payne-Aldrich Bill of 1909, for example, flaxseed was 25 cents a bushel, 20 cents a bushel in the Underwood-Simmons Bill of 1913, and a proposed 40 cents a bushel in the Fordney-McCumber Bill. Lemons were 1.5 cents per pound in 1909, 5 cents per pound in bulk in 1913 and 2 cents per pound in the new proposal. Beef would be 3 cents and lamb 4 cents a pound in 1922, while beef was only 1.5 cents and lamb was a mere 2 cents in 1909. Corn was one of the few products that had stayed the same in both the 1909 and 1922 bills at 15 cents a bushel.[82]

On July 1, the Senate agreed to the duty of 30 cents a bushel on wheat dictated by the farm bloc. Underwood declared that this increased rate on wheat, the highest ever (it was 25 cents in the Payne Bill of 1909), would impose an increased tax of approximately $100 million a year on the American people and benefit the farmers of only three states. McCumber defended the duty on behalf of the farmer after just learning of his failure to be renominated. He said:

For twenty three years and over, I have been fighting the battle for the interests of the farmers of my state. I think my efforts in holding up the tariff rates have been worth hundreds of millions in the years of my service to the people of my state. I shall close my labors just fighting their battles and still attempting to secure for them all that I can possibly secure by a tariff bill in adding to the value of their products. And when I leave the Senate, I hope to leave it with a good protection upon the wheat of the North Dakota farmer."[83]

On July 7, the Republican leadership once again attempted to stop debate on the tariff bill by imposing closure. However, as before, closure was defeated. Five Republicans, joined with the Democrats to vote against closure. The final vote was 45 for closure and 35 against--nine votes short of the necessary two-thirds.[84]

Toward the end of July, McCumber once again found himself the center of controversy. The senator from North Dakota continued his attacks on the press, claiming that the Publishers Association in 1912 had demanded that unless newsprint was placed on the free list, they would oppose President Taft in his reelection bid. When the Senate Finance Committee refused to make any such bargain, the association, did indeed refuse to support the president. Robinson called McCumber's assertion ludicrous, while Don C. Seitz, the business manager of the *New York World*, went further by claiming that most papers in 1912 had supported Taft over Roosevelt and Wilson. Seitz declared, "This talk of Senator McCumber is merely part of the imbecility and ignorance that has been shown by Senator McCumber and his colleagues in framing the present tariff bill."[85] McCumber claimed that he was misquoted. He never meant to say that newspaper threats were the cause of President Taft's defeat in 1912. What he really meant was that the newspapers, by their criticism of the president, split the party and encouraged the Roosevelt candidacy.[86]

On July 27, Senator Lenroot of Wisconsin offered an amendment to limit the wool tariff to 60 percent ad valorem. The wool lobby opposed the amendment, which was defeated. As a result, Democratic Senator Thaddeus Carraway of Arkansas called for an investigation into a linkage of wool rates and all the financial interests of all senators. He alleged that senators in the sheep business voted for high wool rates to enhance the value of their own properties.[87]

On August 3, Republican Senator Charles Gooding of Idaho, a leader of the farm bloc as well as a sheep owner, successfully delayed Carraway's investigation. At the same time, he called on the Senate to look into the motives of all the tariff bill's critics. For example, Gooding wanted to investigate all the senators who published newspapers that had editorially criticized the pending tariff bill or that had accepted advertisements or subsidies from individuals or business concerns in the importing business and from department stores.[88]

On August 19, 1922, the Senate voted in favor of the McCumber Bill by 48 to 25. The only Republican to vote against the bill was Borah. Norris and LaFollette were paired against it, while Lenroot and Kellogg, severe critics of the bill, voted for it. Only three Democratic senators favored this law. John Kendrick of Wyoming and Joseph Ransdell and Edwin Broussard of Louisiana. Both Ransdell and Broussard were influenced by the sugar interests in their state and were happy to see the duties raised to $2.30 per pound for world sugar and to $1.84 per pound for Cuban sugar. This was considerably higher than the Underwood rate of $1.26 per pound and the Emergency Bill of $2.00 per pound.[89]

The Republicans praised their handiwork by declaring that the new tariff would raise customs revenue by $408 million, $70 million more than the Underwood Bill, and would create many new jobs in the United States. McCumber proudly stated that the main consideration in framing the bill was to stabilize American labor and to protect labor from ruinous foreign competition. From the Republican point of view, this was the best tariff bill of all.[90]

The opponents of the new tariff bill, including the *New York Times*, predicted that the implementation of this bill would lead to a Republican disaster at the polls in the November elections. According to a *New York Times* editorial entitled "Robbing the Consumer," only eight Republican senators had voted against the duties on cutlery reaching 118 to 225 percent. Consequently, the *Times* argued that the increased prices of spoons, forks, and knives would be felt by every American household. "Makers of these tariffs are making Democratic voters every day.... What economic, what political genius must have been spent in the concoction of a tariff that stirs in Republicans a burning desire for Republican defeat"![91]

Four days after the Senate voted on the McCumber Bill, a conference committee was appointed, comprised of five members of each chamber, to reconcile the differences between the House and Senate versions of the tariff bill. Fordney led the House delegation with fellow Republicans William Green of Iowa and Nicholas Longworth (son-in-law of Theodore Roosevelt) of Ohio and Democrats John Nance Garner of Texas and James Collier of Mississippi. McCumber led the Senate delegation, which included Republicans Smoot and McLean and Democrats Simmons and Artemis Jones of New Mexico. The committee had to deal with over 2,436 Senate amendments to the House bill.[92]

From August 28 to September 9, the committee remained deadlocked over one issue--the valuation plan. Fordney remained insistent that the American Valuation Plan be implemented, and he opposed the Senate compromise of giving the president power to raise or lower rates within certain limits. At the same time, Smoot opposed the American Valuation, claiming that it would cause inflation throughout the country. This deadlock gave the Democrats the opportunity to accuse the Republicans of purposefully delaying the bill until after the November elections.[93]

On September 9, a major breakthrough occurred, and the conference committee reached agreement on a tariff bill. For the most part, the Senate version of the bill was adopted as high rates on agricultural goods were retained along with foreign valuation. It was a major victory for the farm bloc and for McCumber. For example, the tariff on wheat in the House version was 25 cents a bushel, while it was increased to 30 cents a bushel in the Senate. The conference committee agreed on the Senate version. The resolution of the battle over wool was also closer to the Senate than House version. The House tariff on wool was put at 25 cents a pound, while the Senate raised it to 33 cents a pound. The committee compromised on 31 cents a pound. Sugar rates in the House version were higher for world sugar at $2.00 per pound and only $1.60 per pound for Cuban sugar. The Senate version increased both rates in the following manner: world sugar rates were raised to $2.30 per pound, while Cuban sugar rates were increased to $1.84 per pound. Once again, the conference committee settled closer to the Senate version as world sugar rates were established at $2.20 per pound and Cuban sugar rates at $1.76 per pound.[94]

As mentioned above, agreeing on the type of tariff valuation had been the major difficulty in obtaining a compromise measure between the House and the Senate. Fordney refused to relent on American valuation, and the Senate conferees led by Smoot, on this issue, favored foreign valuation. As it turned out, foreign valuation was accepted and the House conferees agreed to the elastic tariff provision that gave the president authorization, under certain limitations, to change the tariff rates after an investigation by the Tariff Commission. This provision, in itself, would not have satisfied Fordney; however, the conference committee, after much debate, reached a compromise that allowed the president to employ the American Valuation Plan in changing the rates if deemed advisable by the Tariff Commission. This persuaded him to accept the Senate plan.[95]

The farm bloc and the influence of the chemical lobby in the conference committee were responsible for restoring the dye embargo and a $30 a ton duty on potash. The dye embargo became an integral part of the Emergency Tariff legislation in 1921, and its lobby had unsuccessfully attempted to continue it in the Fordney-McCumber Tariff. Neither the House nor the Senate version included it. Thus, it was somewhat of a surprise to find that the conference committee had restored it for one year from the effective date of the new tariff and had given the president the right to continue it longer by proclamation.[96]

On September 13, the House of Representatives received the conference report and prepared to vote on it. House Democrats opposed the report, joined by 102 Republicans who demanded that the dye embargo be eliminated and fertilizer potash be put on the free list. The textile lobby, in particular, fought against restoring the dye embargo, fearing that it would add to the cost of their goods. To the dismay and agitation of the Republican party leaders, the House voted 177 to 130 to recommit the conference report.[97]

On September 14, the Republican leaders surrendered to the tariff bolters, dropped the dye embargo, and returned potash to the free list. The leadership had no choice, for there was too much dissension in the House over the dye embargo. To do anything else would play into the hands of the Democrats and delay the bill indefinitely. McCumber especially was unhappy about the revolt in the House. On leaving the conference room, he referred to the action taken as a "shameful surrender." Turning to Fordney, he once again blamed the press for the revolt in the House when he said, "Did you tell the newspapermen that they all turned Democrats."[98]

The next day, the House, wishing to adjourn the following week and to prepare for the November elections, voted 210 to 90 to accept the revised report, eliminating both the dye embargo and the duty on potash. Garner attempted to have the whole bill resubmitted in order to reduce the high sugar rates to their more respectable 1913 level. He tried unsuccessfully to gain the Republican's support by warning them that higher sugar duties would mean higher prices and almost certain defeat at the polls in November.[99]

On September 16, the Senate met to discuss and vote on the revised Conference Committee Bill. Both Underwood and Simmons attempted to block the vote on the bill, claiming that the conferees exceeded their authority. Underwood, the Democratic floor leader, opposed the provision of the bill that gave the president the right to substitute American valuation for foreign valuation in connection with any of the schedules. This provision, he argued, created an entirely new tariff bill that provided more protection than either of the earlier House and Senate versions. Since this was new legislation, it should be returned to both chambers for further review. Simmons assailed the bill, declaring that it would hurt both workers and consumers and only benefit the profiteers.[100]

On September 20, the Senate voted 43 to 28 to support the revised Conference Committee report and passed the tariff bill. The only five Republicans who voted against it were Borah, Ralph Cameron of Arizona, Cummins, LaFollette, and Lenroot. Norris was listed as absent but opposed. The only two Democrats to support the measure were the two Louisianans, Broussard and Ransdell. The Democrats continued to charge that the new rates were higher than those in any other previous tariff bill, and the end result would be the undermining of foreign trade, along with an increase in the cost of living for most Americans.[101]

On September 21, President Harding signed the Fordney-McCumber Tariff Act. He called it one of the greatest tariff bills ever created by Congress and assured the American people that it would contribute to a growing prosperity in the United States. While the president signed the bill, ships were hurrying to ports and importers were withdrawing goods worth millions of dollars to escape higher rates [102].

When Harding signed the tariff bill, McCumber was a lame duck, defeated two months earlier in the North Dakota Republican primary. He was also an increasingly embittered man, as noted by some of his

statements on the floor of the Senate as he complained about the way in
which the newspapers were criticizing his efforts. His comments
suggested a man who was not accustomed to being in the political
spotlight.[103]

McCumber's loss was viewed in Washington with alarm and
concern. Some later historians have noted that he was a victim of a
phenomenon not entirely unknown in American politics--a midterm revolt
against incumbents, regardless of party. In North Dakota, however, the
defeat did not come as a surprise. He was under considerable criticism
for being a "reactionary in Washington and a radical at home," a charge
perhaps made more believable by the leadership he was displaying in
piloting the tariff bill through the Senate.[104] While he still insisted on
provisions to aid the farmers of his state, the general complexion of the
bill was such that many progressive politicians from agricultural states
were critical of it.

McCumber's loss was not entirely due to his support for the tariff
and his reputation. He might have obtained the support of a new
moderate group that had emerged in the early 1920s in opposition to the
Non-Partisan League. The Independent Voters Association (IVA) was
certainly close to McCumber on the issues but it could not support him.
First, they saw him as being too close to the League. He had never
taken a hard stand against it, nor had it opposed him, in spite of his call
for patriotism during the war and his economic conservatism. And there
was his growing aloofness from the voters in North Dakota.
Specifically, he was criticized for his sponsorship of one Andrew Miller
for a federal judgeship, a nomination that encountered considerable
criticism in the state. When confronted by the IVA on the matter, he
assumed a haughty attitude and told critics that he would only appear
before them to read a statement on the subject and would not answer
questions on the nomination.[105]

Perhaps more important than even this episode was the fact that the
two men most responsible for his reelection in 1916, Alexander
McKenzie and Arthur Townley, had passed from the scene and could no
longer help him. Townley was on the outs with many of those who had
previously idolized him, and the machine that he had built up was
beginning to turn against him. When the League met to consider whom
it would endorse, Townley spoke up for the nomination of the state's
senior senator. He used the phrase "balance of power," meaning that
there was one League-endorsed radical (Ladd) and one conservative
(McCumber) in the Senate from North Dakota and that that equation
should be preserved. To the audience, the thought of endorsing the
"reactionary" McCumber was unthinkable. As a result, the man who
had led the grass-roots revolt of the farmers and who had brought terror
into the corridors of many state capitols was himself now the victim of

a grass roots revolt as well. The convention rejected his proposal. Nor would they have anything to do with Asle J. Gronna, who was considering a comeback in 1922. The man whom they would ultimately nominate was the politically martyred ex-Governor Lynn Frazier.[106]

Alexander McKenzie was still part of the North Dakota political picture in the period after the war, although his power in no way approached the clout he wielded during the early part of the twentieth century. He still had his fingers in many projects in the state and though semiretired, had played a role in the 1920 presidential election. By 1922 his most important asset was his access to money and influence, and it was this qualification that made McCumber's prospects fairly strong. However, in January of that year, shortly after his longtime ally became chairman of the Senate Finance Committee, McKenzie died, having made but one brief trip to the nation's capital in order to try to get the monies necessary to fight off what would be the most serious challenge of the Senator's career.[107]

McCumber announced his bid for reelection in March, 1922, laying considerable emphasis on his support for federal legislation to regulate the grain trade, a point that had always impressed those voters who voted with the Non-Partisan League.[108] He also emphasized his support for a system of cooperative marketing with provisions for terminal markets in large cities to eliminate the "middlemen" as much as possible. He had introduced a bill to set up such a system in January of that year.[109] McCumber also called for a decrease in the interest charges on mortgages and other debts. In the spring of 1922, however, much of his emphasis was on what he had become. He talked about his new role as chairman of the Senate Finance Committee and how it would help the state of North Dakota as well as about his identity as a "true Republican" and a careful progressive" and not a socialist. He told his constituents that the high protective tariff would benefit agricultural states in the Midwest as well as the industrial states of the East.[110]

Yet arguing for himself as one who was firmly rooted in the ranks of the Senate establishment had its drawbacks. First, 1922 would be a bad year for incumbents as the general dissatisfaction with the Harding administration led to the punishment of those senators and representatives of both parties who were seen as "establishment" figures. Second, it was not a good reputation for anyone running in North Dakota. While the Non-Partisan League might have been on the downward spiral, its message of challenge to the established interests was still strong. The spirit of what North Dakota had become was the candidacy of the farmer-politician Lynn Frazier, who had been turned out of the governor's mansion by conservative interests. The state's ideal was not a man who had served twenty-four years in the Senate, who had held positions of power and influence, and who was probably more at home in the living room of Henry Cabot Lodge than that of a North Dakota farmer.

The results of the election, then, were less surprising to most North Dakotans then they were to the newspapers in the East. Initially, it appeared that McCumber had won, as the big cities of the state reported first--Fargo, Bismarck, Grand Forks, and Minot. Here was where the senator hoped to pile up a sufficient majority to overcome what he knew would be strong support for Frazier in agricultural regions.[111] However, when the strong returns for the former governor began to come in from the rural areas, the senator knew he was beaten. He had received a 2 to 1 margin in the cities, but as it turned out, he needed a 4 to 1 edge as Frazier piled up a 15,000 vote advantage when all the votes were counted. That it was a personal loss for McCumber was made all the more obvious when the gubernatorial candidate backed by the Non-Partisan League lost to the incumbent.

The Democrats rejoiced in Frazier's victory, even though they knew that in a one-party state such as North Dakota it would have no meaning for them. The Democratic National Committee called it a rebuke to Harding and to conservative Republicanism. Some suggestions were made that McCumber might lead a bolt of moderate Republicans out of the party and support the Democratic nominee, but the senator quickly put a stop to that. McCumber announced that he would back Frazier. He had his own explanation as to why he had lost. He wrote his campaign manager that the two months during which the campaign had taken place were just too short to counteract the "poison" that had been spread by the Non-Partisan League. He suggested that perhaps he had been the victim of a bipartisan effort, noting that the Democrats had supported Frazier and that some of them had crossed party lines.[112]

As noted earlier in this section, McCumber was in Washington when the returns came in that signalled the end of his political career. However, he still had almost eight months left on his term during which he would shepherd the tariff bill and the veterans' bonus bill through the Congress. So, he remained in Washington. He was not too pleased when his colleague Ladd, who had supported Frazier, rejoiced in the triumph, calling Frazier a product of the new school of politics and his senior colleague part of the old.[113]

There were other issues to deal with as well. By his own definition, McCumber was still the champion of the small farmer, and he told the Senate in early 1923 that the Congress should develop legislation to further cooperative selling. He also wanted a program by which certain products would be withheld from the markets as a means of driving up the price of agricultural products. He did not have too much faith in other proposals to resolve agricultural problems, including those that would extend agricultural credits. These bills, he said, only scratched the surface. He was not too optimistic about talk of the "farmer-labor" coalition which some in the farm bloc were beginning to advocate. If the farmers got the wages they wanted, prices would go up and labor unions would complain mightily.[114]

One of McCumber's last efforts showed him to be a man who understood the politics of the pork barrel, a device by which each legislator adds a "hometown" amendment on to a general appropriations bill--in this instance, a rivers and harbors bill. His contribution was designed to develop commerce north of Sioux City on the Missouri River. It would aid commerce, he told his colleagues, because the railroad terminals were located there and the project would facilitate the transportation of goods harvested in North Dakota. There was some chicanery in this proposal because rivers and harbors bills were designed to facilitate water commerce, not rail commerce.[115]

Following his defeat, McCumber did not leave Washington to go back to North Dakota. He practiced law in the capital from 1923 until 1925, thus following a precedent set by so many of his colleagues who had lost office. He became affiliated with several law firms in Washington and then, in 1925,[116] he accepted an appointment from President Coolidge to the International Joint Commission which had been created by a treaty to pass on all cases involving use of the boundary waters between the United States and Canada. He remained on this body until his death in May of 1933.

What happened after Porter McCumber's death is significant in terms of the type of criticism that was leveled at him during his last campaign. The man who had grown so far from his midwestern roots that he had lost touch with his constituents, and eventually lost his position as a result, did not go back to the state he had represented in the Senate even in death. His funeral was held in Washington, and he was interred in the Abbey Mausoleum adjoining Arlington National Cemetery. In death as in life, McCumber remained closer to Washington and the seat of power than to the farmers and the farms of North Dakota.

In November, 1922 Frank Taussig, writing in *The Quarterly Journal of Economics*, began what would become years of criticism of the Fordney-McCumber Tariff Act. Taussig, the leading American expert on tariffs, opposed protection in general, contending that it ran counter to sound economic principle. He concentrated his criticism on the "flexible" provision of the tariff act that gave the president the power to implement either American or foreign valuation. Taussig stated that in order for the president to impose changes in the tariff act, the Tariff Commission had to find out the foreign costs of production. This was impossible, however, since foreign countries would not permit such scrutiny of their books. Therefore, any figures obtained from abroad would be inaccurate and untrustworthy--unlike the United States where firms employ uniform records of cost accounting and accountants scrutinize every item of expense.[117]   His was only one of a series of criticisms.

The Fordney-McCumber Bill had set the highest tariff rates known up to that time. It was a repudiation of the Underwood-Simmons Tariff and a return to the high protective policies of the Dingley and Payne bills. In fact, the Payne Bill was used as a basis, and in a large number of cases, the duties imposed in that law were renamed in the Fordney-McCumber Tariff. Reductions below the rates prevailing in the Underwood-Simmons Bill in 1913 were very few. Some articles or materials imported in moderate quantities were transferred from the dutiable to the free list in the Underwood law. This brought it under fire from any economist who rejected protectionist arguments.

The schedules in which the rates of the Payne-Aldrich Tariff were followed were for textiles, cotton, woolens, silks, linens, earthenware, glassware, and some agricultural products. For example, in the case of cotton sewing thread, the Underwood Bill called for a 15 percent ad valorem, the Payne-Aldrich a 20 percent, and the Fordney-McCumber 20 to 35 percent. The same principle applied to cotton cloth, which rose slightly in the Fordney-McCumber Bill. The Underwood rate was 7.5 to 30 percent ad valorem, the Payne-Aldrich 15 to 40 percent, and the Fordney-McCumber 20 to 45 percent. In the case of raw wool, the Fordney-McCumber figure was slightly under that of Payne-Aldrich. The Payne-Aldrich Bill called for 33 cents a pound for raw wool, the Fordney-McCumber figure was 31 cents and in the Underwood Bill, raw wool had been placed on the free list. In the case of sewing silk, both the Payne-Aldrich and Fordney-McCumber figures were the same at $1.50 a pound. In the Underwood Bill, sewing silk had been established at 15 percent ad valorem.[118]

Rates raised above the Payne Bill in the Fordney-McCumber Tariff were for chemicals, especially coal tar products, certain manufactured articles like cutlery, clocks (including the infamous cuckoo clock referred to in Chapter 1), china, toys, a considerable range of agricultural products, and several minerals and alloys used in metallurgical operations. Arguments on these last mentioned articles were frequent in the Senate. Those who supported the higher than Payne rates did so on the grounds that excessive competition from abroad would destroy many new American industries that began during the war. These arguments were also raised concerning rates in the new chemical industry. Before World War I, Germany had been the chief source of supply of coal tar dyes. Because this source was cut off during the war, the United States had to invest in its own chemical industry.

Investment in this industry rose rapidly during the war, increasing from a mere $3 million in 1918 to about $174 million in 1921. Once the war was over, it became important to protect the United States' huge investment from German competition. The German chemical industry was more advanced, with more experts and greater knowledge of secret processes. The United States could not expect to compete with them on an equal footing; therefore, it became imperative to keep their goods out of the American market. In fact, the protectionists wanted to continue the embargo in the Emergency Tariff Act of 1921 against dyes, coal tar products and other goods used in the chemical industry.

The opponents of both a high tariff and an embargo pointed out that the American chemical industry only came into existence as a result of the outright theft of German patents that the U.S. government had seized during the war an sold at bargain rates to American industries. In the end, the Senate refused to continue the embargo of the Emergency Tariff, but raised rates so high as to have the same effect as an embargo. For example, dyes, synthetic chemicals and explosives, and products of coal tar in the intermediate state were fixed at 20 percent ad valorem in the Payne-Aldrich Bill, 15 percent in the Underwood Bill and 7 cents a pound plus 55 percent ad valorem, based on American evaluation, in the new Fordney-McCumber Bill. Comparing the various rates for coal-tar finished products, there was little difference. The Payne-Aldrich rate was raised to 40 percent ad valorem, and the Underwood to 40 percent, and the Fordney-McCumber maintained the same 7 cents per pound but a 60 percent ad valorem in addition, based on American evaluation. [119]

The protectionists noted the large profits made by a few importers of such articles as razors, cutlery, clocks, and toys. McCumber complained that many of these goods were overpriced in the American market owing to the cost of transportation, handling, and insurance. Using this argument, the senator from North Dakota had been instrumental in raising the rates of many of the above items. For example, straight razors in the Payne-Aldrich Bill were fixed at 35 percent ad valorem to 15 cents each plus 35 percent, the Underwood rates were 35 percent to 55 percent and the Fordney-McCumber rates were established at 18 cents each plus 45 percent to 45 cents each, plus 45 percent. In the case of clocks, the Payne-Aldrich rate was 40 percent ad valorem, the Underwood 30 percent, and the Fordney-McCumber 45 percent. McCumber produced a razor that cost a mere 21 cents abroad while the same razor sold for $5 in the United States. The cuckoo clocks, which made such a hit on the Senate floor, cost 94 cents in Germany and $22 in the United States. Some might argue that, by allowing these goods to enter the American market, the domestic manufacturers of these goods were endangered. American manufacturers could easily undercut their foreign competition by selling the goods under the European price in the United States, thus negating the need to impose a tariff.[120]

The increase in the rates on raw sugar was one of the most controversial in the entire bill. The duty on world raw sugar had been fixed at $1.68 per pound (Cuban raw sugar at $1.76 per pound) in the Payne-Aldrich Bill, $1.25 per pound in the Underwood bill (Cuban raw sugar was only 1 cent per pound), and $2.20 per pound in the Fordney-McCumber Bill (Cuban raw was $1.76 per pound). Interestingly, there was a large public outcry when it came to high sugar duties. For example, when world sugar rates climbed to $2 a pound in the Emergency Tariff of 1921, public resentment increased, and it was expected that sugar rates would be reduced in the Fordney-McCumber Bill. However, the power of the sugar cane lobby in Louisiana and the sugar beet lobby in California, Michigan, Colorado, and Utah prevailed over the wrath of the public in shaping that part of the Fordney-McCumber Act.[121]

Probably the most controversial of all the rates increased in the Fordney-McCumber Tariff were those pertaining to ores, metals, and alloys. These materials were used in the manufacture of steel, and prior to the war they had all been imported. During the war both demand and price increased as supply decreased. When the war ended, an increase in the supply of imported ores would have brought the price down, and American manufacturers wanted to protect the high price of their metals and ores by putting them on the protective list. The argument for doing so was not so much to keep the price artificially high as to ensure that the United States would always have on hand a large supply of these crucial materials in the event of another war. Thus, tungsten ore, ferrotungsten, and manganese ore--all considered important to the national defense of the country and to the economic welfare of U.S. industry--were more protected than before. In the Payne-Aldrich Bill, the rate for tungsten ore had stood at 20 percent ad valorem; in the Underwood Bill, it was placed on the free list; and in the Fordney-McCumber Bill, the figure imposed was 45 cents per pound of contained tungsten. Ferrotungsten stood at 25 percent ad valorem in the Payne-Aldrich Bill and 15 percent in the Underwood Bill and jumped to 60 cents per pound of contained tungsten plus 25 percent.[122]

The tariff rate on manganese ore was among the most vigorously debated rates. Practically all high-grade manganese ore before the war had come from India, Russia, and Brazil. This ore was used in the production of ferromanganese, an alloy needed to produce soft steel. In both the Payne-Aldrich and Underwood bills, manganese ore occupied the free list. However, the final version of the Fordney-McCumber Tariff granted the manganese ore producers a rate of 1 cent per pound on manganese contained in all grades of this mineral having a metal content in excess of 30 percent. In analyzing the prices of minerals after the war, this duty was equivalent to an ad valorem rate of about 50 percent.[123]

Because of the farm bloc's efforts, the Fordney-McCumber Bill protected the farmer with the highest rates ever imposed on his goods. This had been a particular concern of McCumber's. Below are listed the tariff rates on certain agricultural goods in the Payne-Aldrich, the Underwood-Simmons and the Fordney-McCumber tariff acts.[124]

	Payne	Underwood	Fordney
Poultry	0.03 a pound	Free	0.03 a pound
Eggs	0.05 a dozen	Free	0.08 a dozen
Corn	0.15 a bushel	Free	0.15 a bushel
Oats	0.15 a bushel	0.06 a bushel	0.15 a bushel
Rye	0.10 a bushel	Free	0.15 a bushel
Rolled Oats	0.01 a pound	0.30 per 100 pounds	0.80 per 100
Olives	0.15 a gallon	0.15 a gallon	0.20 a gallon
Wheat	Free	Free	0.30 a bushel
Apples	0.25 a bushel	0.10 a bushel	0.25 a bushel
Apricots	Free	Free	0.5 a pound
Lemons	0.015 a pound	0.5 a pound	0.02 a pound
Potatoes	0.25 a bushel	Free	0.50 per 100
Peanuts	0.01 a pound	0.01 a pound	0.04 a pound
Butter	0.06 a pound	0.025 a pound	0.08 a pound

In 1916 during the Wilson administration, a bipartisan tariff commission had been created as a technical information body designed to advise the Congress in framing the tariff. Originally, this body had no regulatory or even advisory power. However, with the passage of the Fordney-McCumber Bill, the commission now had the responsibility of helping the president determine differences in the cost of production at home and abroad. On the commission's recommendation, the president might raise or decrease any duty as much as 50 percent in order to adjust the difference between U.S. and foreign costs of production. A section of the Fordney-McCumber Bill stated that the United States Tariff Commission now had the power to conduct "investigations to assist the president in ascertaining differences in costs of production....the Commission shall give reasonable public notice of its hearings and shall give reasonable opportunity to parties interested to be present, to produce evidence, and to be heard."[125]

The president was not bound by the commission's recommendations; he could circumvent the cost of production rule completely if the customary rule did not permit an adequate increase in the rates. Under these circumstances, the president might impose the American evaluation as the basis of his calculations. This highly involved procedure would provide a sliding tariff scale so that duties could go up without an act of Congress when extra protection was needed and down when rates were found to be too high. These flexible schedules would not work well in practice during the next six years of the Harding-Coolidge administrations, and during that time the bipartisan commission grew excessively protectionist and made few recommendations of consequence. Harding and Coolidge together instituted only thirty-seven changes, thirty-two of which called for higher rates. The five items on which they lowered the duties were relatively insignificant in terms of the American market. Duties were lowered on millfeeds, bobwhite quail, paintbrush handles, cresylic acid and phenol. A recommendation of the commission in 1924 that President Coolidge should lower the duty on sugar was ignored when the sugar lobby raised objections.[126]

In conclusion, the Fordney-McCumber Tariff raised rates higher than any protective measure had up to that time. It considerably increased the rates of the Underwood-Simmons Tariff, and it installed what was intended to be a flexible tariff to equalize the cost of U.S. and foreign goods to the domestic consumer. Most economic historians agree that the Fordney-McCumber Tariff probably did more harm than good for both the national and international economy in the 1920s, for it gave little stimulation to most of the industries that had expanded rapidly after the war. It did not apply to the automobile industry, which grew rapidly in the postwar period, and it failed to protect both agricultural and textile prices which fell rapidly in the 1920s. On the other hand, like most protective tariffs, the Fordney-McCumber Bill reduced competition to the extent that most nonfarm prices remained artificially high until the onset of the Depression. The industry that benefited most from the tariff was the chemical industry, which grew rapidly in the 1920s. However, the growth of the chemical industry probably owed more to the fact that it fell heir to German patents during the war than the tariff after the war.

The Tariff Act had a strong effect on the international economy. During World War I, many European nations, primarily Great Britain and France, had borrowed large sums of money from the United States, which the United States expected to be repaid. However, with the passage of the new tariff bill, it became difficult, if not impossible, for many European nations to sell their goods in the United States and thus make much of the necessary revenue to repay their war loans. The high tariff also caused European nations to retaliate by raising their tariffs and thus keeping American goods from entering the European market. This was particularly difficult for American farmers because they needed to export their large surpluses.

The Tariff Commission made no provision to investigate the effect of duties on the export trade of the United States. A proposed amendment to the Fordney-McCumber Bill would have mandated the commission "to investigate the operation of customs laws, including their relation to federal revenue, and their effect upon the export commerce, the industries, and the labor of the country."[127]   However, the protectionists, already having given the commission more power than it had in 1916, defeated the amendment.[128]

Porter McCumber is perhaps as representative of the economic nationalists of this period as might be found in American politics. While we might be tempted to say that he was fundamentally an internationalist, based on his commitment to international law and his support of the League of Nations, in other matters pertaining to foreign affairs he supported the nationalist view reflected in his posture on Mexico, the Philippines, the prosecution of the war, and the Canadian Reciprocity Treaty. Even when arguing for compensation to Colombia for the loss of Panama, he contended that to do so would be to further American economic and political interests in the hemisphere. The picture of McCumber as a nationalist on both foreign policy and domestic questions would appear to be accurate. It is appropriate that a tariff that epitomized economic nationalism bore his name.

McCumber's economic nationalism, as reflected in his position on the tariff, is also shown in the positions of those senators and representatives who generally supported high tariff policies during this period. McCumber's insistence on ensuring that farm products, specifically those that were native to North Dakota, is also very much in character with most of his fellow protectionists. The picture of McCumber as a "western man with eastern ideas," or as a "conservative in a progressive state" does not tell the full story.

This remark is true only if we can isolate McCumber from other midwestern legislators of this period and show that his position on the tariff and on other protectionist legislation was significantly different from that of other senators and representatives from farm states. Most of them, relatively obscure figures at best, do not appear to vary distinctly from McCumber on most relevant matters. Only a few of them, such as Norris and LaFollette, remain as vivid figures, defying party loyalty and Republican orthodoxy as embodied in the high tariff position. For most, protest of eastern-oriented tariff legislation was more a political than an economic posture.

In short, McCumber can be seen as a typical figure of the period in his support of protectionist policies, fiscal orthodoxy, and party loyalty. He is also typical of legislators who are more in touch with the views of their constituents than is commonly thought. The rise of the Non-Partisan League and its prominence in North Dakota politics contributed to McCumber's eventual defeat, but we must ask just how much of a factor it was, and to what extent the League differed with him on the basic issues, particularly those addressed in this study. The Non-Partisan League, like McCumber, spoke for the small farmers of the Middlewest, and there is no evidence that it had any argument with him on his tariff position. Their argument with him was on other matters, and there is the additional consideration that he was not one of them. Furthermore, the older Non-Partisan League leaders, who could have "lived with McCumber," had been shouldered aside in a power struggle. McCumber and other victims of the League were rejected because of who they were rather than because of what they stood for. Otherwise, why would the League have rejected Asle Gronna, whose career seemed the antithesis of McCumber's?

McCumber's economic nationalism, then, is representative of the dominant party of his time, of the political climate of his state, and of the American population during this period. It is the picture of him and the circumstances of his defeat that has created a false impression of his role in history. Given the bias of history books, his association with a piece of legislation that is the epitome of protectionism, followed by his defeat, leaves a wrong impression of what he truly represented.

What happened in 1922 was part of a political process that had become inevitable with the United States' changeover from an agricultural to an industrial society. As the demand for protectionism grew stronger, parties vied for the opportunity to cash in on the situation in order to gain political capital. McCumber supported the policy, partly out of a sense of nationalism and partly out of a belief that an economic policy dedicated to the growth of business served all the country. He spearheaded the effort of the farmers, whose political influence was dying, to share in the consequences of a protectionist policy.

NOTES

1. See Elwyn Robinson, *History of North Dakota* (Lincoln: University of Nebraska Press, 1966) pp. 327-370 for material covering this period. For McCumber's role in the party see William Widener, "Henry Cabot Lodge" in Richard Baker and Roger Davidson, eds., *First Among Equals* (Washington: Congressional Quarterly, 1991), p. 53; See also Ronald Feinman, *Twilight of Progressivism: Western Republicans and the New Deal* (Baltimore: John Hopkins Press, 1981), pp. 10-11.

2. Belle and Fola LaFollette, *Robert M. LaFollette, June 14, 1855-June 18, 1925* (New York: Macmillan Co., 1953), pp. 1021-1024; *New York Times*, June 30, 1922, p. 1.

3. *New York Times*, June 30, 1922, p. 1.

4. Robinson, p. 259, and *New York Times*, March 9, 1914, p. 19 and October 1, 1918, p. 1.

5. *New York Times*, October 9, 1921, pp. 1-2.

6. Ibid., November 13, 1921, p. 10.

7. Ibid., March 25, 1922, p. 2.

8. John Chalmers Vinson, *The Parchment Peace* (Athens, Ga.: University of Georgia Press, 1955), pp. 146-149 and 198-199.

9. Abraham Berglund, "The Tariff Act of 1922," *American Economic Review* 13 (March, 1923): 15.

10. F. W. Taussig, *The Tariff History of the United States* (New York: G. P. Putnam's Sons, 1910), pp. 447-448.

11. Berglund, pp. 14-15.

12. *New York Times*, January 13, 1921 p. 1 and February 12, 1921, p. 6.

13. Ibid., January 14, 1921, p. 21 and January 18, 1921, p. 3.

14. Ibid., February 22, 1921, p. 20; March 4, 1921, p. 1; *Congressional Record*, 67th Congress, 1st Session, pp. 1288-1289; Arthur S. Link, "What Happened to the Progressive Movement in the 1920's," *American Historical Review*, 64 (July, 1959): 851-883.

15. *New York Times*, February 22, 1921, p. 20.

16. Ibid., February 25, 1921, p. 15; February 27, 1921, p. 5; March 1, 1921, p. 17; March 4, 1921, p. 1.

17. Ibid., February 22, 1921, p. 20; March 4, 1921, p. 1; May 5, 1921, p. 5.

18. Ibid.

19. Ibid., May 1, 1921, p. 5; May 12, 1921, p. 1; May 14, 1921, p. 8; May 19, 1921, p. 17; May 28, 1921, p. 2.

20. Ibid., May 30, 1921, p. 8.

21. Ibid., June 10, 1921, p. 12; June 14, 1921, p. 20; June 15, 1921, p. 8; June 21, 1921, p. 16.

22. Ibid., June 29, 1921, p. 2; June 30, 1921, p. 1.

23. Ibid.

24. Ibid., July 15, 1921, p. 15; July 16, 1921, p. 3; June 30, 1921, p. 8.

25. Ibid.

26. Ibid., July 1, 1921, p. 2; July 8, 1921, pp. 1-2; July 10, 1921, p. 3.

27. Ibid., July 2, 1921, p. 2.

28. Ibid., July 22, p. 1.

29. Ibid., July 18, p. 10.

30. Ibid., July 23, 1921, p. 14; July 26, 1921, p. 3; July 28, 1921, p. 3; July 31, 1921, p. 6.

31. Ibid., July 26, 1921, p. 3; August 12, 1921, p. 3.

32. Ibid., August 10, 1921, p. 4; August 12, 1921, p. 3.

33. Ibid., August 28, 1921, p. 20; September 2, 1921, p. 12.

34. Ibid., August 31, 1914, p. 15; December 19, 1921, p. 27; December 21, 1921, p. 12.

35. Ibid., November 16, p. 3.

36. Ibid., November 7, 1921, p. 16; November 9, 1921, p. 11; November 16, 1921, p. 17.

37. Ibid., December 5, 1921, p. 32.

38. Ibid., November 18, 1921, p. 28; December 22, 1921, p. 6.

39. *New York Times*, January 2, 1922, p. 1; Henry Ashurst, *A Many Colored Toga: The Diary of Henry Fountain Ashurst* (Tucson: University of Arizona Press, 1962), pp. 156-157 and 164-165.

40. Francis Russell, *The Shadow of Blooming Grove: Warren G. Harding and His Times* (New York: McGraw-Hill, 1968), p. 433.

41. Quoted in Ron Chernow, *House of Morgan* (New York: Atlantic Press, 1990), p. 128.

42. *New York Times*, January 2, 1922, pp. 1-3.

43. Ibid., January 9, 1922, p. 14.

44. Ibid., January 10, 1922, p. 19.

45. Ibid., January 15, 1922, VII, p. 3.

46. Ibid.

47. Ibid., March 1, 1921, p. 23; March 3, 1921.

48. Robert Murray, *The Politics of Normalcy* (New York: W. W. Norton, 1973), p. 72.

49. *New York Times*, April 26, 1922, p. 12.

50. Ibid., May 6, 1922, p. 1; May 7, 1922, p. 1.

51. Russell, p. 534.

52. *New York Times*, February 17, 1922, p. 2.

53. Ibid., June 16, 1922, p. 1.

54. Ibid., June 17, 1922, p. 1.

55. Ibid., September 16, 1922, p. 1.

56. Murray, pp. 74-75.

57. Russell, p. 550 and Murray, pp. 72-74. See the New York Times, September 21, 1922, p. 1.

58. New York Times, September 22, 1922, p. 1.

59. Ibid., January 10, 1922, p. 18.

60. Ibid.

61. Ibid., January 11, 1922, p. 23.

62. Ibid., January 20, 1922, p. 26; January 21, 1922, p. 20.

63. Ibid., February 19, 1922, p. 19.

64. Ibid., March 16, 1922, p. 9.

65. Ibid., April 1, 1922, p. 8.

66. Ibid., April 11, 1922, p. 8.

67. Ibid., April 11, 1922, p. 8; April 12, 1922, p. 1.

68. Ibid., April 12, 1922, p. 15; April 13, 1922, p. 1.

69. Ibid.
70. Ibid., May 1, 1922, p. 19; April 14, 1922, p. 19.
71. Ibid., May 2, 1922, p. 18.
72. Ibid., May 5, 1922, p. 19.
73. Ibid., May 2, 1922, p. 18.
74. Ibid., May 9, 1922, p. 18.
75. Ibid., May 11, 1922, p. 19.
76. Ibid.
77. Ibid., May 15, 1922, p. 1; May 18, 1922, p. 21.
78. Ibid., May 26, 1922, p. 21; May 28, 1922, p. 3.
79. Ibid., June 2, 1922, p. 1.
80. Ibid., June 16, 1922, p. 16 and p. 19.
81. Ibid., June 25, Section II, p. 1.
82. Ibid., June 28, 1922, p. 2; Berglund, 22; Taussig, p. 455.
83. *New York Times*, July 2, 1922, p. 1.
84. Ibid., July 8, 1922, p. 1.
85. Ibid., July 27, 1922, p. 7.
86. Ibid., July 28, 1922, p. 15.
87. Ibid., July 27, 1922, p. 19; July 30, 1922, p. 1.
88. Ibid., August 3, 1922, p. 17; August 4, 1922, p. 1.
89. Ibid., August 19, 1922, p. 1; August 20, 1922, p. 1.
90. Ibid., August 19, 1922, p. 1; August 20, 1922, p. 2.
91. Ibid., August 19, 1922, p. 10.
92. Ibid., August 23, 1922, p. 26.
93. Ibid., August 23, 1922, p. 13.
94. Ibid., September 10, 1922, p. 1.
95. Ibid.
96. Ibid., September 11, 1922, p. 1.
97. Ibid., September 11, 1922, p. 1; September 14, 1922, p. 1.
98. Ibid., September 15, 1922, p. 1.
99. Ibid., September 16, 1922, p. 1.
100. Ibid., September 17, 1922, p. 20; September 19, 1922, p. 7.
101. Ibid., September 20, 1922, p. 1.
102. Ibid., September 22, 1922, p. 1; *Congressional Record*, September 21, 1922 (67th Congress).
103. Ibid., June 16, 1922, p. 16.
104. *New York Times*, June 12, 1922, p. 17.
105. Robert Morlan, *Political Prairie Fire: The Non-Partisan League* (Minneapolis: University of Minnesota Press, 1955), p. 342.
106. *New York Times*, March 27, 1922, p. 4; W. W. Phillips, "Asle J. Gronna: Self-Made Man of the Plains," Ph.D. thesis, University of Missouri, 1958, pp. 665 et seq.

107. David Baglien, "The McKenzie Era: A Political History of North Dakota from 1880-1920," M.A. thesis, North Dakota State University, 1955, pp. 151-153.

108. *New York Times*, March 21, 1922, p. 21.

109. Ibid., January 25, 1922, p. 3.

110. Ibid., March 21, 1922, p. 21.

111. Ibid., June 29, 1922, p. 1.

112. Ibid., June 30, 1922, p. 1; July 1, 1922, p. 4.

113. Ibid.

114. Ibid., February 2, 1923, p. 14.

115. Ibid., February 10, 1923, p. 12.

116. *New York Times*, June 1, 1925, p. 21.

117. Frank Taussig, "Tariff Act of 1922," *Quarterly Journal of Economics* 37 (November, 1922): 1-28; *New York Times*, December 18, 1922, p. 16.

118. *New York Times*, September 13, 1922, p. 12.

119. Ibid., p. 12.

120. Ibid., p. 12; Berglund, pp. 22-23.

121. *New York Times*, September 13, 1922, p. 12.

122. Berglund, p. 25.

123. Ibid., pp. 22-26.

124. *New York Times*, September 13, 1922, p. 12.

125. Berglund, p. 31.

126. Taussig, pp. 481-486.

127. Berglund, p. 32.

128. Ibid.

Bibliography

BOOKS

Ambrosius, Lloyd. *Woodrow Wilson and the American Diplomatic Tradition.* Middlesex: Cambridge Press, 1987.

Anderson, Donald. *William Howard Taft, A Conservative's Conception of the Presidency.* Ithaca, N.Y.: Cornell University Press, 1968.

Ashurst, Henry. *A Many Colored Toga; The Diary of Henry Fountain Ashurst.* Tucson: University of Arizona Press, 1962.

Bailey, Thomas. *Woodrow Wilson and the Great Betrayal.* New York: Macmillan Co., 1945.

_____. *Woodrow Wilson and the Lost Peace.* New York: Macmillan Co., 1944.

Baker, Richard, and Davidson, Roger. *First Among Equals.* Washington, D.C.: Congressional Quarterly, 1991.

Bowers, Claude. *William Beveridge and the Progressive Era.* Boston: Houghton, 1932.

Burdick, Usher. *Farmer Political Action in North Dakota.* Baltimore: Wirth Bros., 1944.

Butler, Nicholas Murray. *Across the Busy Years*. Vol. 1. New York: Charles Scribner and Sons, 1939.

Chernow, Ron. *The House of Morgan*. New York: Atlantic Press, 1990.

Cole, Wayne. *Senator Gerald P. Nye and American Foreign Policy*. Minneapolis: University of Minnesota Press, 1962.

Cooper, John Milton. *The Vanity of Power: American Isolationism and World War I*. Westport, Conn.: Greenwood Press, 1969.

Cranston, Alan. *The Killing of the Peace*. New York: Viking Press, 1945.

Crawford, Lewis. *A History of North Dakota*. Vol. 1. Chicago: American Historical Society, 1931

Ellis, L. Ethan. *Reciprocity 1911: A Study in Canadian-American Relations*. New Haven, Conn.: Yale University Press, 1939.

Feinman, Ronald. *Twilight of Progressivism: The Western Republicans and the New Deal*. Baltimore: Johns Hopkins Press, 1981.

Ferrell, Robert. *Woodrow Wilson and World War I, 1917-1921*. New York: Harper and Row, 1985.

Finnegan, John. *Against the Spectre of the Dragon*. Westport, Conn.: Greenwood Press, 1974.

Fite, Gilbert, and Reese, James. *An Economic History of the United States*. Boston: Houghton, 1973.

Fleming, Denna. *The United States and the League of Nations, 1918-1920*. New York: Russell and Russell, 1932.

Garraty, John. *Henry Cabot Lodge, A Biography*. New York: Alfred A. Knopf, 1953

Glad, Betty. *Key Pittman: The Tragedy of a Senate Insider*. New York: Columbia University Press, 1986.

Goldman, Eric. *Rendezvous With Destiny*. New York: Alfred A. Knopf, 1953.

Grantham, Dewey. *Hoke Smith and the Politics of the New South*. Baton Rouge: Louisiana State University Press, 1958.

Gray, James H. *R. B. Bennett, The Calgary Years*. Toronto, Canada: University of Toronto Press, 1991.

Holt, James. *Congressional Insurgents and the Party System*. Cambridge, Mass.: Harvard University Press, 1967.

Hutchison, Bruce. *The Incredible Canadian*. New York and Toronto: Longman Greens, 1953.

Johnson, Evan. *Oscar W. Underwood*. Baton Rouge: Louisiana State University Press, 1980.

Karfunkel, Thomas, and Ryley, Thomas. *The Jewish Seat: Anti-Semitism and the Appointment of Jews to the Supreme Court*. Hicksville, N.Y.: Exposition University Press, 1978.

LaFollette, Belle and Fola. *Robert M. LaFollette, June 14, 1855-June 18, 1925*. 2 vols. New York: Macmillan Co., 1953.

Larson, Bruce. *Lindbergh of Minnesota*. New York: Harcourt Brace Jovanovich, 1971.

Leech, Margaret. *In the Days of McKinley*. New York: Harper Brothers, 1959.

Link, Arthur S. *Wilson: The New Freedom*. Princeton, N.J.: Princeton University Press, 1956.

_____. *Woodrow Wilson and the Progressive Era*. New York: Harper and Row, 1945.

Lodge, Henry Cabot. *The Senate and The League of Nations*. New York: Charles Scribner's Sons, 1925.

Margulies, Herbert. *The Mild Reservationists and the League of Nations Controversy in the Senate*. Columbia: University of Missouri Press, 1989.

_____. *Senator Lenroot of Wisconsin, A Political Biography*. Columbia: University of Missouri Press, 1977.

McKenna, Marion. *Borah*. Ann Arbor: University of Michigan Press, 1961.

McNaught, Kenneth. *The Penguin History of Canada*. Middlesex: Penguin Books, 1969.

Merrill, H. S. *Bourbon Leader: Grover Cleveland and the Democratic Party*. Boston: Little, Brown, 1957.

Morlan, Robert. *Political Prairie Fire: The Non-Partisan League*. Minneapolis: University of Minnesota Press, 1955.

Mowry, George. *The Era of Theodore Roosevelt*. New York: Harper and Brothers, 1958.

_____. *Theodore Roosevelt and the Progressive Movement*. Madison: University of Wisconsin Press, 1946.

Murray, Robert. *The Politics of Normalcy*. New York: W. W. Norton, 1973.

Neuberger, Richard, and Kahn, Stephen. *Integrity: The Life of George W. Norris*. New York: Vanguard Press, 1937.

Nevins, Allan. *Grover Cleveland*. New York: Dodd Mead, 1934.

Norris, George. *Fighting Liberal*. New York: Macmillan Co., 1945.

Nye, Russell. *Midwestern Progressive Politics*. East Lansing: Michigan State University Press, 1959.

Peterson, H. C. and Fite, Gilbert. *Opponents of War: 1917-1918*. Madison, Wisconsin: University of Wisconsin Press, 1957.

Phillips, D. G. *The Treason of the Senate*. Chicago: Quadrangle Books, 1964 (reprint).

Primm, James. *The American Experience*. Vol. 2. Saint Charles, Mo.: Forum Press, 1973.

Robinson, Elwyn. *History of North Dakota*. Lincoln: University of Nebraska Press, 1966.

Russell, Francis. *The Shadow of Blooming Grove: Warren G. Harding and His Times*. New York: McGraw-Hill, 1968.

Ryley, Thomas. *A Little Group of Willful Men*. Port Washington, N. Y.: Kennikat, 1975.

Shull, Robert. *Laurier: The First Canadian*. New York and Toronto: Macmillan Co., 1965.

Stone, Ralph. *The Irreconcileables*. Lexington: University of Kentucky Press, 1970.

Taussig, F. W. *The Tariff History of the United States*. New York: G. P. Putnam Sons, 1910.

Thelen, David. *Robert M. LaFollette and the Insurgent Spirit*. Boston: Little, Brown, 1976.

Towne, Ruth Warner. *Senator William J. Stone and the Politics of Compromise*. Port Washington, N. Y.: Kennikat, 1979.

Tuchman, Barbara. *The Zimmermann Telegram*. New York: Macmillan Co., 1966.

Vinson, John Chalmers. *The Parchment Peace*. Athens, Ga.: University of Georgia Press, 1955.

Walton, Gary, and Robertson, Ross M. *History of the American Economy*. New York: Harcourt Brace Jovanovich, 1983.

Widener, William. *Henry Cabot Lodge and the Search for An American Foreign Policy*. Berkeley: University of California Press, 1980.

UNPUBLISHED DISSERTATIONS

Baglien, David. "The McKenzie Era: A Political History of North Dakota from 1880-1920." M.A. thesis, North Dakota State University, 1955.

Carey, Kenneth. "Alexander McKenzie: Boss of North Dakota." M.A. thesis, University of North Dakota, 1949.

Glaab, Charles. "John Burke and the North Dakota Progressive
     Movement." M.A. thesis, University of North Dakota, 1952.

Morrison, Paul. "The Position of Senators from North Dakota on
     Isolation, 1889-1920." Ph.D. thesis, University of Colorado,
     1954.

Norman, Richard. "The Election of 1912 and the Progressive Party of
     North Dakota." M.A. thesis, University of North Dakota,
     1950.

Phillips, W. W. "Asle J. Gronna: Self Made Man of the Plains." Ph.D.
     thesis, University of Missouri, 1958.

ARTICLES

Berglund, Abraham. "The Tariff Act of 1922." *American Economic
     Review* 13 (March, 1923): 14-32.

Darling, H. M. "Who Kept the United States Out of the League of
     Nations." *Canadian Historical Association* 10 (1929):
     196-211.

Glaab, Charles. "North Dakota vs. McKenzie." *North Dakota Quarterly*
     (Fall, 1956): 103-111.

_____. "The Failure of North Dakota Progressivism." *Mid-America*
     (October, 1957): 195-200.

Link, Arthur S. "What Happened to the Progressive Movement in the
     1920s?" *American Historical Review* 64 (July, 1959):
     851-883.

Taussig, Frank. "Tariff Act of 1913." *Quarterly Journal of Economics*
     28 (1913): 1-30.

_____. "Tariff Act of 1922." *Quarterly Journal of Economics* 37
     (November, 1922): 1-28.

Index

Adamson Act, 30
Agricultural Committee, 68
Agricultural Workers' Union, 70
Aldrich Bill, 41-43
Aldrich, Nelson, 25-26, 41-43,
   45, 107
American Valuation, 103-107,
   111-112, 117-118
Anti-Dumping, 101
Armed Ship Bill, 64-66, 68
Article X, 79, 85, 88-89, 91
Ashurst, Henry, 14, 50, 63

Beach, Rex, 25
Beveridge, William, 25, 41-42
Blaine, James G., 3
Borah, William, 42, 62, 78, 80,
   84-86, 98, 116, 119
Borden, Sir Robert, 47
Brandegee, Frank, 78, 80-81, 85
Brandeis, Louis, 30
Bristow, Joseph, 41-42
Broussard, Edwin, 116, 119
Bryan, William Jennings, 57-58
Burke, John, 17, 20, 22, 27-28,
   32, 47-48, 60-61, 70, 96

Butler, Nicholas Murray, 84

Cameron, Ralph, 119
Canadian Reciprocity Treaty,
   16, 30, 32, 45, 47-48, 129
Cannon, Joseph, 29-30, 32,
   40, 43
Carraway, Thaddeus, 116
Casey, Lyman, 21
Chamber of Commerce, 105-106
Chicago Board of Trade, 69
Choate, Joseph, 57
Claiborne, Charles, 111
Clapp, Moses, 41
Clark, Champ, 45-46
Cleveland, Grover, 1, 4-6,
   8-9
Collier, James, 117
Colt, LeBaron, 79, 84
Coolidge, Calvin, 123-128
Culberson, Charles, 25
Cummins, Albert, 42, 50

Dakota Farmer's Alliance, 19
DePew, Chauncey, 25
Dingley, Nelson, 9-10

Dingley Tariff, 9-10, 12, 39,
    41, 44, 99, 124
Dolliver, Jonathan, 41-42

Emergency Tariff Bill, 99,
    101-102, 104-106, 108,
    116, 118, 125-126
Esch, John, 97
Esch-Cummins Act, 97

Fall, Albert, 78, 90
Farm Bloc, 111
Federal Trade Commission,
    30
Foraker, Joseph, 25
Fordney Bill, 103-106, 111-112
Fordney, Joseph, 100, 103-104,
    107, 110-112, 117-119
Fordney-McCumber Tariff,
    introduction, debate and
    passage, 103-122; analysis of
    the bill, 123-130
Frazier, Lynn, 68, 96, 121-122

Garner, John Nance, 104, 117,
    119
Gompers, Samuel, 70
Gooding, Charles, 116
Gore, Thomas, 58-59, 68
Gore-McLemore Resolution, 59
Gorman, Arthur, 5
Grain Grading Act, 28
Grangers, 45
Green, William, 117
Gronna, Asle, 12-14, 17, 21,
    26-27, 29-33, 47-48, 55, 57,
    61-63, 65-68, 76, 78, 82,
    87, 97, 121, 130

Hague Conference, 56-57, 60
Hale, Eugene, 45
Hanna, Louis, 32-33, 47-48,
    60-61
Hanna, Mark, 4, 20, 25
Hansbrough, Henry, 9, 12, 22,

    24, 26-27, 30-31
Harding, Warren, 79, 84-85,
    91, 99, 101-103, 105,
    109-112, 119, 121-122,
    128
Harrison, Benjamin, 4
Helgesen, Henry, 46-48,
    55, 67
Hellstrom, Frank, 47-48
Hepburn Act, 26
Hepburn, William, 29
Hill, James J., 24
Hitchcock, Gilbert, 17, 30,
    57-58, 62-64, 66, 71,
    76-78, 81-91, 102,
    113-114
Hoover, Herbert, 105
Huerta, Victoriano, 56
Hughes, Charles Evans, 61,
    98, 106
Hull, Cordell, 51

International Workers of
    the World, 70, 89
Irreconcilables, 76, 78-79,
    84, 88, 90-91

Johnson, Hiram, 64, 78-79, 82,
    86
Johnson, Martin, 9, 22-23, 27,
    31, 44
Jones, Artemis, 117
Jones, Wesley, 62

Karger, Gus, 79, 84
Kellogg, Frank, 78-79, 82, 84,
    90-91
Kendrick, John, 116
Kenyon, William, 78, 82, 98
Kirby, John, 111
Kitchin, Claude, 59, 104
Knox, Philander, 78, 81, 83,
    85, 90

Ladd, Edwin, 97, 112-113, 120,

122
LaFollette, Robert, 12, 21, 26,
   30, 33, 46-47, 51, 62-63,
   66-67, 76, 78, 82, 97-98,
   116, 119, 129
LaMoure, Judson, 23
Langer, William, 96
Lansing, Robert, 62-63, 69
Laurier, Sir Wilfred, 44-45, 47
League of Nations, 55, 57, 62,
   68, 75-84, 86, 88-91
Lemke, William, 96
Lenroot, Irvine, 116, 119
Little, C. B., 23
Lodge, Henry Cabot, 25-26,
   40-42, 62, 64, 66, 71,
   77-82, 84-91
Longworth, Nicholas, 117
Lusitania, 58-59

Marshall, Thomas, 27, 31-32
Marshall, Thomas R., 82
McCumber, Annie Fuller,
   mother of Porter J.
   McCumber, 17
McCumber, Jennie Scharnig,
   wife of Porter J. McCumber,
   17
McCumber, Orlin, father of
   Porter J. McCumber, 17
McCumber, Porter J., early
   career, 13-33; position on
   early twentieth-century tariff
   bills, 44-48, 51; U.S. foreign
   policy, 55-71; Treaty of
   Versailles, 75-91; tariff bills
   of the 1920s, 102, 107-110,
   112-123, 129-130. See also
   the Emergency Tariff Bill and
   the Fordney-McCumber Tariff
McKenzie, Alexander, 13-14,
   17-32, 44, 61, 96, 120-121
McKinley Tariff, 1-9, 12
McKinley, William, 1-4, 7,
   9-10, 12, 20, 24-25

McLean, George, 114, 117
McLemore, Jeff, 58
McNary, Charles, 79, 82, 84,
   90
Meat Inspection Bill, 29
Mellon, Andrew, 107, 109
Miller, Andrew, 120
Morgan, J. P., 107
Monroe Doctrine, 79-80

Nelson, Knute, 25, 79, 82, 91
Newberry, Truman, 97-98
Non-Partisan League, 52, 55,
   60-61, 67-70, 75-76, 96-97,
   107, 120-122, 129-130
Norris, George, 13, 26, 30,
   62, 65-67, 76, 78, 82, 98,
   116, 119, 129
North Dakota politics, 15-32,
   44-47, 52, 55, 60-61, 64,
   67, 75-76, 96-97, 120-122
Norton, Patrick, 47-48
Noyes, Arthur, 24

O'Gorman, James, 58, 63-64

Payne-Aldrich Tariff, 26, 39,
   43-45, 48, 51, 100-104,
   111, 115, 124-127
Payne Bill, 40-43, 50
Payne, Sereno, 40
Penrose, Boies, 25, 77-78,
   100, 102, 105-108
Perkins, George, 25
Pierce, Gilbert, 21
Platt, Orville, 25
Populist Party, 5, 12
Purcell, William, 32
Pure Food and Drug Act, 14,
   32, 107

Quay, Matthew, 25

Ransdell, Joseph, 116, 119
Reed, James, 63, 78

Reed, Thomas, 5, 10, 50
Richland County, 17-19, 23
Roach, William, 9, 12, 22-23
Roosevelt, Theodore, 20, 29, 32,
    39, 41, 47-48, 60
Root, Elihu, 84

Sarles, Elwood, 27
Seitz, Don, 116
Shantung, 84-86, 89
Sherman Anti-Trust Act, 5
Sherman, Lawrence, 81
Shields, John, 78-87
Ship Purchase Bill, 57-58
Simmons, Furnifold, 49-50,
    101-102, 112-114, 117, 119
Sinclair, James, 104
Sinclair, Upton, 29
Smoot, Reed, 112, 117-118
Soldier Bonus Bill, 108-110,
    122
Spalding, Burleigh, 27
Standard Oil Company, 5
Stone, William Joel, 45-46,
    58-59, 62-67
Sussex Pledge, 58, 62-63
Swanson, Claude, 85

Taft, William Howard, 14,
    39-44, 46-48, 77, 79, 84,
    89, 116
Taussig, Frank, 102, 123
Thompson, Fountain, 32
Tillman, Ben, 25
Townley, Arthur, 52, 61,
    96-97, 120

Underwood, Oscar, 40-41, 44,
    46, 49
Underwood-Simmons Tariff,
    48, 51-52, 99-100, 103,
    112, 115, 124, 127-128
United States Tariff Commission,
    1, 113, 127

Venezuelan boundary dispute,
    22
Versailles, Treaty of, 75-77,
    90, 98-99
Villa, Pancho, 56

Walsh, Thomas, 50, 113, 115
Warren, Francis, 25
Washington Naval Conference,
    98, 106
Weaver, James, 21
White, Henry, 80
Wiley, Harvey, 28
Williams, John Sharp, 46, 56,
    67
Wilson-Gorman Tariff, 5-6,
    8-10
Wilson, William, 5-6
Wilson, Woodrow, 22, 28,
    48-51, 56-64, 66-67, 69-71,
    75-77, 79, 81-91, 97,
    100-102, 109, 113, 116, 127
Winship, George, 27
Woman suffrage, 98-99
World Court, 98

Young, George, 47-48

Zimmermann telegram, 63, 65

About the Authors

EDWARD S. KAPLAN, a Professor with the Social Science Department at New York City Technical College of the City University of New York, teaches Macroeconomics, Microeconomics, Money and Banking, and his specialty, Economic History of the United States. He has written several articles on twentieth century U.S. economic history.

THOMAS W. RYLEY is Adjunct Professor of History and Political Science at Molloy College. He is Professor Emeritus from New York City Technical College of the University of New York. He is the author of *A Little Group of Willful Men* and the co-author of *The Jewish Seat: Anti-Semitism and the Appointment of Jews to the Supreme Court*.